42-5955

The Letters of
JOHN DRYDEN

John Dryden

The Letters of
JOHN DRYDEN

With Letters Addressed to Him

COLLECTED AND EDITED BY

CHARLES E. WARD

AMS PRESS, INC.
NEW YORK

Reprinted with the
Permission of
DUKE UNIVERSITY PRESS

1965

AMS PRESS, INC.
New York, N. Y. 10003

To

D and G

PREFACE

To undertake an edition of the correspondence of John Dryden is more rewarding in the anticipation than in the result. Inasmuch as no serious attempt has been made to assemble and edit the letters since Malone's edition in 1800, it would seem to offer a fair field for one seeking more knowledge about the man. To edit and annotate the letters which have been printed before is indeed a worthy service to Dryden himself. But to find new letters has proved well-nigh impossible. Dryden lived before the days when poets and playwrights wrote letters with one eye on posterity, and indeed before the commercial value of such private correspondence was widely recognized. In consequence, there are relatively few letters—eleven, to be precise—included here which were not printed in previous editions; and all but one of these (Letter 5) have been published in scattered places during the last fifty years. There appears to have been slight disposition on the part of Dryden's friends or relations to treasure up his letters, either for sentiment or for gain. Of the hundreds he must have written during the course of a long literary career, only sixty-two have been preserved. The rest, many of which may well have been superior to those now preserved, have disappeared into the dust bin of time.

Although much is lost, a great deal yet remains. In the present collection are assembled seventy-seven letters, including fifteen from various correspondents to

Dryden. Unfortunately they fall, for the most part, in Dryden's later years. The earliest letter, in point of time, is still that to his cousin, Honor Dryden, written probably while he was an undergraduate at Trinity College, Cambridge, in his early twenties. Nearly a dozen years elapse before the next letter, written in 1664. By this time he was rapidly establishing himself as a poet and a playwright. So in the years during which he must have been experimenting with verse, and finding a livelihood as a government employee, along with Milton and Marvell, we have not a scrap of the personal or the gossipy or the literary. Did he live precariously in London on his inheritance and his small government salary? Did he turn hack to Herringman, as Shadwell years later was to charge? Did he woo Lady Elizabeth Howard in poetic accents, or was he actually hectored into marriage with her in 1663 by her brothers, as was later asserted, again by Shadwell? The answers are perhaps locked up in the letters of those years—the letters which have not yet yielded to the searchers of a hundred and fifty years.

The period of the next twenty years of his life is almost as complete a blank. Two letters, which tell precious little, can be dated between 1664 and 1682. And these two decades, it should be remembered, are extremely important for any adequate interpretation of Dryden's life. In this period he became poet laureate to Charles II; he developed into the great playwright of the time; his family of three boys grew up and went to college; he all but deserted the stage for political satire; and what is specially significant, he was thinking

seriously of religion and philosophy: for *Religio Laici*,
with its implications for his consequent change to the
Roman Catholic faith, appeared in 1682. And the letters of this time? One to the Earl of Rochester, written
from London; another to the Earl of Dorset, written
from the country, both, it will be observed, isolated,
quite unrelated to others. Some of the later letters
(they become more numerous after 1682) come in runs,
but not without many omissions. In this category may be
placed three groups: those to and from Tonson and
Walsh, and to Mrs. Steward. They are, I think, sufficiently varied to offer some interest to the reader. The
Tonson correspondence provides a sort of back-scene
view of the personal and business relations of the poet
and his publisher. The letters in the Walsh group (five
of them published here for the first time) show us
Dryden the friend and mentor of aspiring young literary men. And the letters to Mrs. Steward reveal
another Dryden: the charming, gracious, appreciative
old man talking to a young and devoted relation.

Not many of the letters, I think, are totally without
value to the student of Dryden or of the period. At the
same time it must be said that to the casual reader who
is not a specialist they will probably seem extraordi-
narily dull, though Dryden is anything but a dull man.
The truth would seem to be that Dryden was not at all
concerned with "literary" composition when he sat
down to pen a letter. The interesting topic and the
polished phrase, which are often associated with the
correspondence of literary men, are generally lacking.
Lacking too are the confessions relating to his art: the

inspiration for this poem, the genesis of that, the struggles with another. No, Dryden did not burden his correspondents with critical or esthetic chitchat. Had he talked more about himself and his work, we should doubtless have a far easier task to understand him; the fact remains, however, that though he often mentions the judgment of posterity, he did unconscionably little, on the personal side, to help it form one.

Thin as many of the letters are with regard to biographical details, they form almost the only real source for a study of the man. His age was not given overmuch to literary reminiscence, nor was he. He kept (so far as we are aware) no diary, as did his friend Pepys and his acquaintance Evelyn; few of his contemporaries, except those who put him into satire or lampoon, thought it worth their while to record impressions of Glorious John or Poet Squab or Bayes. Aubrey gives us only a scrap of information in *Brief Lives:* he was awaiting the fulfillment of the poet's promise to supply a sketch of himself, which Dryden never got around to.

Although a few of these letters found their way into the biographical studies of Derrick and of Dr. Johnson,[1] it remained for Edmond Malone to make the first systematic search for letters. For his *Critical and Miscellaneous Prose Works of John Dryden* in 1800, he tapped several sources before then unknown: he gathered the Tonson correspondence, and the letters to Mrs. Steward. In all he printed forty-five letters. His edition has become the source for subsequent editors; and

[1] See James M. Osborn, *John Dryden: Some Biographical Facts and Problems* (New York, 1940), pp. 15-38.

after a century and a half his notes are still of considerable value.

But Malone's accuracy was not so great as his dili-
gence. Without explanation, and often without con-
sistency, he applied his own editorial principles, which
left the texts somewhat mutilated. In copying many
letters, he employed his own system of punctuation and
capitalization, without much regard for Dryden's; in
other letters, he used Dryden's in one portion and his
own in another. Occasionally he dropped out words, or
misread them. In one letter he silently omitted an entire sentence, presumably because it grated upon his
sensibilities. But in spite of these lapses, his edition is
useful; and, in several instances, when I could not find,
or could not obtain, copies or photostats of the originals,
I have relied upon Malone for my text.[2]

When Sir Walter Scott published the complete
Works of John Dryden in 1808, he went to Malone for
the text of the letters. Scott was too busy with a host of
other matters to find hours for the usually unrewarding
search for new material of this kind. He added, however, one document-letter, which I print here in a
corrected form as No. 7.

Nearly a half century passed after Scott's edition before any additional letters were brought to light. These
appeared, not in a new edition of the correspondence,
but in the Introduction to the *Poetical Works of John*

---

[2] Malone projected a second edition of his work, which was never called
for. In preparation for it, he made numerous corrections in the letters and
found a few new ones. Through the kindness of Mr. James M. Osborn I am
able to incorporate Malone's corrections to those letters for which I depend
upon him.

Dryden (1854) by Robert Bell. With the help of
Charles Beville Dryden, Bell was able to print for the
first time a letter to Walsh (here Letter 17), and Dryden's note on the reverse side of Charles Dryden's letter
to Mrs. Steward (here Letter 66); and four more
which he discovered in the Middlehill Collection of Sir
Thomas Phillipps. When one remembers the scarcity
of Dryden letters, Bell's contribution seems considerable. Furthermore, Bell was a careful transcriber; his
texts show little of the irregularity of Malone's practices.

Since Bell, only one letter was added to the corpus
before the present century; this is Letter 56 in the
present edition. It appeared in 1858 in the *Illustrated
London News*, contributed by a person who signed himself, curiously enough, a "well-wisher." In his revision
of Scott, Saintsbury seems to have made little or no
effort to unearth new letters,[3] he made no changes in
the text, and added nothing of importance to the notes.

With its admitted faults, the Malone edition remains
the best aid to the modern editor. His notes, used by
both Scott and Saintsbury, were superseded by neither.

In preparing the present edition I have followed the
practice of earlier editors in printing not only Dryden's
letters but also those addressed to him. Of the latter
there are fifteen. The most notable are those from
Walsh; they are of interest in themselves and they
illumine some of Dryden's which heretofore have been
somewhat obscure. With a few exceptions, all noted in
the headnotes to the several letters, I have been able to

---

[3] He placed the *Illustrated London News* letter in the appendix volume of
the complete edition rather than with the other letters; for he was uncertain
of its authenticity.

establish a text by the use of photostats of the original, or by copies which I believe are trustworthy. They are here printed as Dryden wrote them, with all the vagaries of spelling, punctuation, and expression. The present whereabouts of the individual letters I have indicated in the notes, with a statement concerning the place of their first appearance, if hitherto published. Changes and corrections made by the writers I have relegated to the bottom of the page of the text and indicated them by the use of lower-case letters. I have generally tried to avoid *sic*, but occasionally I have employed it to protect myself.

Many of the letters, of course, are not dated. For these I have usually accepted Malone's conjectural date unless I could offer a better one. The superscriptions, when I have been able to find them, duly appear at the end of the letter.

The number and extent of explanatory and illustrative notes in such an edition have presented, as they always must, a problem. I have tried to interpret and to illustrate the text, and to incorporate the latest scholarship on Dryden, or on persons and events ancillary to him. To some the notes will doubtless seem too full; to others, somewhat thin. In either case I can only beg indulgence.

In editing the letters for this book I have contracted many obligations, the greatest of which is that to the American Council of Learned Societies. Their grant of a fellowship enabled me to spend the academic year 1935-36 in England, where a considerable amount of

the material here presented was assembled. I am in-
debted also to the British Museum, the Bodleian
Library, the Lambeth Palace Library, the Pierpont
Morgan Library, the William Andrews Clark Memo-
rial Library, the Historical Society of Pennsylvania, the
Harvard College Library, the Haverford College Li-
brary, the R. B. Adam Library, and the Folger
Shakespeare Library.

I am happy to record here also my thanks to many
individuals for their kindnesses: to the Most Honourable the Marquess of Crewe, the Marquess of Downshire, Lord Sackville, Admiral Sir Lewis Clinton-
Baker, Mr. Oliver R. Barrett, Mr. Percy Dobell, Mr.
James M. Osborn, and Percy D. Mundy, Esq. My
particular obligations to each appear in the notes. No
worker in Dryden material can fail to record his debt
to Edmond Malone for his remarkably thorough
researches, nearly a century and a half ago.

C. E. W.

CONTENTS

ILLUSTRATIONS

The Letters of
JOHN DRYDEN

Letter 1

DRYDEN TO HONOR DRYDEN

Madame,

If you have received the lines I sent by the reverend Levite,[1] I doubt not but they have exceedingly wrought upon you; for beeing so longe in a Clergy-mans pocket, assuredly they have acquired more Sanctity then theire Authour meant them. Alasse Madame, for ought I know they may become a Sermon ere they could arrive at you; and believe it having you for the text it could scarcely proove bad, if it light upon one that could handle it indifferently. But I am so miserable a preacher that though I have so sweet and copious a sub-ject, I still fall short in my expressions And instead of an use of thanksgiveing I am allways makeing one of comfort, that I may one day againe have the happinesse to kisse your faire hand . but that is a message I would not so willingly do by letter as by word of mouth. This is a point I must confesse I could willingly dwell longer on, and in this case what ever I say you may confidently take for gospell. But I must hasten. And indeed Madame (Beloved I had almost sayd) hee had need hasten who treats of you; for to speake fully to evry part of your excellencyes requires a longer houre then most persons have allotted them. But in a word your selfe hath been the best Expositor upon the text of your own worth, in that admirable Comment you wrote upon

it, I meane your incomparable letter. By all thats good
(and you Madame are a great part of my Oath) it hath
put me so farre besides my selfe that I have scarce patience to write prose: my pen is stealing into verse[2]
every time I kisse your letter. I am sure the poore paper
smarts for my Idolatry, which by wearing it continually
neere my brest will at last bee burnt and martyrd in
those flames of adoration it hath kindled in mee. But I
forgett Madame what rarityes your letter came fraught
with besides words; You are such a Deity that commands worship by provideing the Sacrifice: you are
pleasd Madame to force mee to write by sending me
Materialls, and compell mee to my greatest happinesse.
Yet though I highly vallue your Magnificent presents,
pardon mee if I must tell the world they are but imperfect Emblemes of your beauty; For the white and red
of waxe and paper are but shaddowes of that vermillion
and snowe in your lips and forehead. And the silver of
the Inkhorne if it presume to vye whitenesse with your
purer Skinne, must confesse it selfe blacker than the
liquor it containes. What then do I more then retrieve
your own guifts? and present you that paper adulterated
with blotts which you gave spotlesse?

> For since t'was mine the white hath lost its hiew
> To show t'was n'ere it selfe but whilst in you;
> The Virgin Waxe hath blusht it selfe to red
> Since it with mee hath lost its Maydenhead.
> You (fairest Nymph) are waxe; oh may you bee
> As well in softnesse so as purity;
> Till Fate and your own happy choise reveale
> Whom you so farre shall blesse to make you seale.

Fairest Valentine the unfeigned wishe of yor humble votary,

Jo: Dryden.

Cambridge
May the
To the faire hands
of Madame Honor Dryden
these crave admittance

Letter 2

DRYDEN TO RICHARD SALWEY

Honour^d S^r

    I was this evening with my Deare cosen Salwey,[1] whose feaver thanks be to god I find much abated, yet calling to mind those many sad differences sudden deaths occasion in families, I deemed it my duty out of that sincere affection I owe him and his relations, to be his remembracer as to ye settlement of his estate,[2] to which I found him very inclinable to wch purpose he engaged mee heartily and humbly to beg your pardon for those unbeseeming expressions, the violence of his distempers forced him to vtter, allso he ernestly requests that you will favour him wth your company to morrow betwixt seven and eight of the clock in ye morning and that there may be wth you Mr Leckmore and Mr West, ye latter I have some acquaintance wth, but as to ye former if youl' be pleased to write a word or two to him by this messenger, my man shall carry it to him, be pleased to write where he lodges. I shall send very early to morrow to enquire after my Cosens health, for if he be not pretty well composed, I deeme it very incovenient to disturbe him wth occasions of this nature. I hope S^r you will not putt any other construction on my intentions herein then my sincere desires to serve him your selfe and y^r worthy relations, who shall ever be y^r reddy friend and servant

                                        J Driden.

    These
    For ye much honour^d
    Rich: Salwey Esqr
    at Mr Warings house
    in Gratias Street

Letter 3

DRYDEN TO SIR ROBERT LONG

                                    Aug. 14th. 1666

    Honourd Sir,
        Since you have been pleasd thus farr to give Your self a trouble in our businesse, the whole profit of which we owe originally to you, when you wrought my Lord to Assign the patent,[1] we^a hope you will so much own your former kindnesse as to keep what money you receive for us in your hands till we come up. As for the unreasonable proposition my Lord Berkshyre made,[2] &

    _____
    ^a we *written over* I

writ us^b word that you approv'd it, we^c well know it was only to be rid of his importunityes we^d have sent an Acquittance signd by us both^e with this inclos'd; & a letter which Sir Robert Howard[3] has done us the favour to write to you, on purpose that the money might be receiv'd by no other then your self in whom we absolutely confide, as becomes,

Honourd, Sir,

Your most obliged, &

most obedient Servants

John Dryden.   Elizabeth Dryden.

Letter 4

DRYDEN TO JOHN WILMOT, EARL
OF ROCHESTER

My Lord

I have accusd my self this Moneth together for not writing to you; I have calld my self by the names I deservd of unmannerly and ungratefull: I have been uneasy, and taken up the resolutions of a Man who is betwixt Sinn and Repentance, convinc'd of what he ought to do, and yet unable to do better. At the last I deferrd it so long, that I almost grew hardend in the neglect; and thought I had sufferd so much in your good opinion,

<hr>

^b us *written between the lines above* me, *which is lined through*
^c we *written over* I   ^d we *written over* I
^e us both *written between the lines above* my wife and myself, *which is lined through*

that it was in vain to hope I could redeem it. So dangerous a thing it is to be inclin'd to Sloath, that I must confesse once for all, I was ready to quit all manner of obligations And to receive, as if it were my due, the most handsom Compliment, couchd in the best language I have read, and this too from my Lord of Rochester, without showing my self sensible of the favour. If your Lordship cou'd condescend so farr to say all those things to me, which I ought to have sayd to you, it might reasonably be concluded, that you had enchanted me to believe those praises, and that I ownd them in my silence. Twas this Consideration that mov'd me at last to put off my Idlenesse. And now the Shame of seeing my self overpayd so much for an ill Dedication,[1] has made me almost repent of my Addresse. I find it is not for me to contend any way with your Lordship, who can write better on the meanest Subject than I can on the best. I have onely ingag'd my selfe in a new debt, when I had hop'd to cancell a part of the old one: And shou'd either have chosen some other Patron, whom it was in my power to have oblig'd by speaking better of him than he deserv'd, or have made your Lordship onely a hearty Dedication of the respect and Honour I had for you, without giveing you the occasion to conquer me, as you have done, at my own Weapon. My onely relief is, that what I have written is publique, and I am so much my own friend, as to conceale your Lordships letter. for that which would have given Vanity to any other poet, has onely given me confusion. You see, my Lord, how farr you have pushd me; I dare not own the honour you have done

me, for feare of showing it to my own disadvantage.
You are that Rerum Natura of your own Lucretius,
Ipsa suis pollens opibus, nihil indiga nostri:[2] You are
above any Incense I can give you; and have all the
happinesse of an idle life, join'd with the good Nature
of an Active. Your friends in town, are ready to envy
the leysure you have given your self in the Country:
though they know you are onely their Steward, and
that you treasure up but so much health, as you intend
to spend on them in Winter. In the meane time you
have withdrawn your selfe from attendance, the curse
of Courts. You may thinke of what you please, and
that as little as you please; (for in my opinion), thinking it selfe, is a kind of paine to a witty man; he finds
so much more in it to disquiet, than to please him. But
I hope your Lordship will not omitt the occasion of
laughing at the Great Duke of B—— who is so oneasy
to [him]self by pursueing the honour of Lieutenant
Generall which flyes him, that he can enjoy nothing he
possesses. Though at the same time, he is so unfit to
command an Army, that he is the onely Man in the
three Nations who does not know it. Yet he still picques
him self, like his father, to find another Isle of Rhe in
Zealand:[3] thinkes this dissappointment an injury to him
which is indeed a favour, and will not be satisfyed but
with his own ruine and with ours. Tis a strange quality in a man to love idlenesse so well as to destroy his
Estate by it; and yet at the same time to pursue so vio-
lently the most toilesome, and most unpleasant part of
businesse.[4] These observations would easily run into
lampoon, if I had not forsworn that dangerous part of

wit, not so much out of good nature, But at least from
the inborn vanity of poets.[5] I should show it to others,
and betray my self to a worse mischief than what I do
give my Enemy. This has been lately the case of Etherege, who translateing a Satyre of Boileau's,[6] and
changing the French names for English, read it so often
that it came to their eares who were concernd; and
forc'd him to leave off the design e're it was half fin-
ish'd. Some of the verses I remember.

> I call a Spade a Spade; Eaton[7] a Bully
> Frampton[8] a pimp, and Brother John[9] a Cully.

But one of his friends, imagind those names not hero-
ique enough for the dignity of a Satyre, and changd
them thus.

> I call a Spade a Spade, Dunbar[10] a Bully
> Brounckard[11] a pimp, and Aubrey Vere[12] a Cully.

Because I deale not in Satyre, I have sent Your Lordship a prologue and epilogue which I made for our
players when they went down to Oxford.[13] I heare,
since they have succeeded; And by the event your
Lordship will judge how easy 'tis to passe any thing
upon an University; and how grosse flattery the learned
will endure. If Your Lordship had been in Town and
I in the Country, I durst not have entertain'd you, with
three pages of a letter; but I know they are very ill
things which can be tedious to a man who is fourscore
miles from Covent Garden.[14] Tis upon this Confidence
that I dare almost promise to entertain you with a thousand bagatelles every week; and not to be serious in

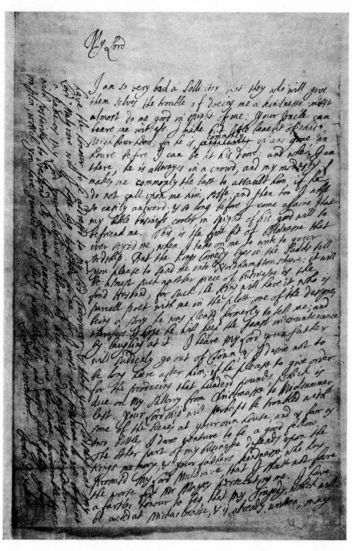

Dryden to Lord [Latimer]

any part of my letter, but that wherein I take leave to call my selfe

> Your Lordships most obedient Servant

Tuesday.   John Dryden.

Letter 5

DRYDEN TO LORD [LATIMER]

My Lord

I am so very bad a Sollicitor, that they who will give them selves the trouble of doeing me a kindnesse, must almost do me good in spight of me: Your Uncle[1] can beare me witness I make but little benefit of his Neighbourhood; for he is commonly*a* up and gone, an houre before I can be at his doore: and when I am there, he is allwayes in a crowd, and my modesty makes me commonly the last to assault him, if he do not call upon me him selfe; and then too I am so easily answerd; & so long before I come againe, that my little business cooles, in spight of his good will to befriend me. This is the first fit of Coldnesse that ever seyzd me, when I take on me to write to your Lordship. But the Kings Comedy lyes in the Sudds till you please to send me into Northamptonshyre: it will be almost such another piece of businesse as the fond Husband, for such the King will have it, who is parcell poet with me

---

a commonly *written above* perpetually, *which is lined through*

in the plott; one of the designes being a story he was pleasd formerly to tell me; and therefore I hope he will keep the jeast in countenance by laughing at it.[2] I heare My Lord your father will suddenly go out of Town; & I desire not to be long heere after him; if he please to give order for the producing that hunderd pounds, which is due on My Sallary from Christmasse to Midsummer, last.[3] Your Lordship will perhaps be troubled with some of the scenes at your own house; and as farr as two bottles I dare venture to be a good fellow. The other part of my businesse depends upon the Kings memory, & your fathers kindnesse, who has promisd My Lord Mulgrave,[4] that I shall not fare the worse for Mr Mayes persecuting me.[5] I have a farther honour to beg, that my Tragedy,[6] which will be acted at Michaelmasse, & is already written, may have the honour to be addressd to My Lord Treasurer; & that your Lordship and My Lord Mulgrave will I hope beg together for me: for I must not presume to use so great a name as My Lord your fathers without his licence; nor do my self that honour with posterity to be[b] reckond his Servant except he will give me the same favourable permission, which you have granted me of being most humbly and most faithfully your Lordships Creature

John Dryden.

---

[b] be *written between the lines*

Letter 6

DRYDEN TO THE EARL OF DORSET

I am now settled in the Country;[1] & haveing given
two or three dayes to idlenesse, parsons, & my Cousin's
discourse, which is the worst of the three evills, am
goeing to drudge for the winter. But Your Lordships
secret[a] is no longer so to me: for, by this tattle which I
have had heere, I am confirmd that there is a certaine
Lady calld Mrs B: Trissham, who is yet at London,
and who is expected down this weeke, without her
Mother.[2] The choice is not amisse; for she is held the
flower of Northamptonshyre: One of the house-mayds
heere has servd her formerly; & my wise cousin[3] should[b]
have married her: but that being broken off, I doubt,
not very handsomely on his side, a breach has[c] ensued;
& I find by him, he is like to marry elswhere ere long.
If your parson's, be not private enough, heere you may
be as unknown as you please, & much more conveniently
then where you design; this house not being above a
little halfe mile distant from the blessed abode; for I
can easily see it from my windowe. and my Cousin is
to be managd As I please; being sufficiently easy as well
in all other things as in his understanding: he talkes
nothing all day long to me in french & Italian to show
his breeding: Mr Rymer sent me his booke, which has
been my best entertainment hetherto: tis certainly very
learned, & the best piece of Criticism in the English

---

[a] secret *written between the lines*
[b] formerly *lined through immediately after* should
[c] has *written above* is, *which is lined through*

tongue; perhaps in any other of the modern.[4] If I am
not altogether of his opinion, I am so, in most of what
he sayes: and thinke my selfe happy that he has not
fallen upon me, as severely and as wittily as he has
upon Shakespeare, and Fletcher. for he is the only man
I know capable of finding out a poets blind sides: and
if he can hold heere without exposeing his Edgar[5] to be
censurd by his Enemyes; I thinke there is no man will
dare to answer him, or can. I am in paine to know[d]
how your Lordship has your health; though I must not
beg to heare it from you; because I had rather see it
confirmd by my own eyes. I am My Lord

Your Lordship's most obedient humble
Servant.   J Dryden.

By Bringis the Carrier, who lodges at the
Bell in Smithfield: & goes out on Thursday
morning: from Mr Elmes his house at
Lilford.

Letter 7

DRYDEN TO AN UNIDENTIFIED PERSON

The two verses, concerning which the dispute is raisd,
are these;

Besides, if o're whatever years prevaile
Shou'd wholly perish, & its matter faile,[1]

The question ariseing from them is, whether any true

[d] know *written over* heare, *which is lined through*

grammaticall construction, can be made of them? The
objection is, that there is no Nominative case appearing,
to the word, Perish: or that can be understood to belong
to it. I have considerd the verses, & find the Authour
of them[2] to have notoriously bungled: that he has
plac'd the words as confus'dly, as if he had studied to
do so. This notwithstanding, the very words without
adding; or diminishing; in theire proper sence, (or at
least what the Authour meanes may run thus.—Besides, if whatever yeares prevaile over, shou'd wholly
perish, & its matter faile.—

I pronounce therefore as impartially as I can upon the
whole, That there is a Nominative case; and that figu-
rative, so as Terence & Virgil amongst others use it.
that is; The whole clause precedent[a] is the Nominative
case to perish. My reason is this; & I thinke it obvious;
let the question be askd, what it is that shoud wholly
perish? or that perishes? the answer will be, that which
yeares prevaile over. If you will not admit a clause to
be in construction a Nominative case; the word (thing)
illud, or quodcung, is to be understood; either[b] of
which words, in the femine [*sic*] gender, agree with
(res) so that he meanes, whatever thing time prevailes
over shou'd wholly perish & its matter faile.
Lucretius, his Latine runs thus:

Praeterea, quae cung vetustate amovet aetus,
Si penitus perimit, consumens materiem omnem,
Unde Animale genus, generatim in lumina vitae
Redducit Venus? &

[a] precedent *written between the lines*
[b] although *before* either *lined through*

Which ought to have been translated thus:

> Besides, what ever time removes from view,
> If he destroys the stock of matter too,
> From whence can kindly propagation spring
> Of every creature, & of every thing?

I translated it*c* (whatever) purposely; to show, that (thing) is to be understood; which as the words are heere plac'd, is so very perspicuous, that the Nominative case cannot be doubted.

The*d* word, perish, usd by Mr Creech is a verb neuter; where Lucretius puts (perimit) which is active: a licence, which in translating a philosophicall Poet, ought not to be taken, for some reasons, which I have not room to give. But, to comfort the looser, I am apt to believe, that the cross-grain, confusd verse put him so much out of patience, that he wou'd not*e* suspect it of any sence.

Sir

The company haveing done me so great an honour, as to make me their judge, I desire from you the favour, of presenting my acknowledgments to them; & shou'd be proud to heare from you, whether they rest satisfy'd in my opinion, who am, Sir Your most humble Servant

John Dryden.

---

c it *written between the lines*
d But *lined through immediately before* The
e looke *lined through immediately after* not

Letter 8

DRYDEN TO THE REVEREND MR. BUSBY

Honourd Sir

We have with much ado recoverd my younger sonn,[1] who came home extreamly sick of a violent cold, & as he thinkes him selfe, a chine-cough. The truth is his constitution is very tender; Yet his desire of learning, I hope, will inable him to brush through the College. He is allwayes gratefully acknowledging your fatherly kindnesse to him; & very willing to his poore power, to do all things which may continue it. I have no more to add, but onely to wish the Eldest may also deserve some part of your good opinion; for I believe him to be of vertuous & pious inclinations; & for both I dare assure you, that they can promise to them selves no farther share of my indulgence, then while they carry them selves with that reverence to you, & that honesty to all others as becomes them. I am

Honourd Sir
Your most Obedient Servant
and Scholar
John Dryden.

Wednesday morning.

For The Reverend
Doctor Busby,
This.

Letter 9

DRYDEN TO THE REVEREND MR. BUSBY

Sir

If I could have found in my selfe a fitting temper, to have waited on you, I had done it, the day you
dismissd my sonn from the College:[1] for he did the
message; and, by what I find from[a] Mr Meredith,[2] as
it was deliverd by you to him: namely that you desird
to see me; and had somewhat to say to me concerning
him. I observ'd likewise somewhat of kindnesse in it,
that you sent him away, that you might not have occasion to correct him. I examin'd the business; and found
it concernd his haveing been Custos[3] foure or five dayes
together. But if he admonishd, and was not believd
because other boyes combind to discredit him with false
witnesseing, and to save them selves, perhaps his crime
was not so great. Another fault it seemes he made
which was goeing into one Hawkes his house with some
others; which you hapning to see, sent your servant to
know who they were; and he onely returnd you my
sonns name: so the rest escapd: I have no fault to find
with my sonns punishment; for that is and ought to be
reserv'd to any Master, much more to you who have
been his fathers. But your man was certainly to blame
to name him onely; and tis onely my respect to you,
that I do not take notice of it to him. My first rash
resolutions were to have brought things past any com-
posure, by immediately sending for my sonns things

[a] from *written above* by, *which is lined* **through**

out of the College: but upon recollection I find I have
a double tye upon me not to do it. one my obligations
to you for my Education: another my great tender-
nesse of doeing anything offensive to my Lord Bishop
of Rochester,[4] as cheife Governour of the College. It
does not consist with the honour I beare him and you, to
go so precipitately to worke: no not so much as to have
any difference with you, if it can possibly be avoyded.
Yet[b] As my sonn stands now, I cannot see with what
credit he can be elected: for being but sixth, and (as
you are pleasd to judge,) not deserving that neither, I
know not whether he may not go immediately to Cambridge, as well as one of his own Election went to Oxford this yeare by your consent.[5] I will say nothing of
my second sonn, but that after you had been pleasd to
advise me to waite on my Lord Bishop for his favour,
I found he might have had the first place, if you had
not opposd it: and I likewise found at the Election, that
by the paines you had taken with him, he in some sort
deservd it: I hope, Sir, when you have given your selfe
the trouble to read thus farr, you, who are a prudent
man, will consider, that none complaine, but they desire
to be reconcild at the same time: there is no mild Ex-
postulation at least, which does not intimate a kindnesse
and respect in him who makes it. Be pleasd if there be
no merit on my side. to make it your own act of grace
to be what you were formerly to my sonn. I have done
something, so farr to conquer my own Spirit as to ask
it: and, indeed, I know not with what face to go to my
Lord Bishop, and to tell him I am takeing away both

[b] Yet *written between the lines*

my sonns: for though I shall tell him no occasion; it
will looke like a disrespect to my old Master; of which
I will not be guilty if it be possible. I shall add no
more, but hope I shall be so satisfyed with a favourable
answer from you, which I promise to my selfe from
your goodnesse and moderation, that I shall still have
occasion to continue
                    Sir
            Your most obliged humble Servant
                    John Dryden.

For The Reverend,
Dr Busby.
This.
[Mr and Mrs Dryden] c

Letter 10

DRYDEN TO LAWRENCE HYDE,
EARL OF ROCHESTER

My Lord
    I know not whether my Lord Sunderland has
interceded with your Lordship, for half a yeare of my
salary: But I have two other Advocates, my extreame
wants, even almost to arresting, & my ill health, which
cannot be repaird without immediate retireing into the
Country. A quarters allowance is but the Jesuites pow-

    c *Added in another hand*

der[1] to my disease; the fitt will return a fortnight
hence. If I durst I wou'd plead a little merit, & some
hazards of my life from the Common Enemyes, my re-
fuseing advantages offerd by them,[2] & neglecting my
beneficiall studyes for the King's service: But I onely
thinke I merite not to sterve. I never applyd myselfe
to any Interest contrary to your Lordship's; and, on
some occasions, perhaps not known to you, have not
been unserviceable to the memory & reputation of My
Lord your father.[3] After this, My Lord, my conscience
assures me I may write boldly, though I cannot speake
to you. I have three sonns growing to mans estate, I
breed them all up to learning, beyond my fortune; but
they are too hopefull to be neglected though I want.[4]
Be pleasd to looke on me with an eye of compassion;
some small Employment wou'd render my condition
easy. The King is not unsatisfyed of me, the Duke[5] has
often promisd me his assistance; & Your Lordship is
the Conduit through which their favours passe. Either
in the Customes, or the Appeales of the Excise, or some
other way; meanes cannot be wanting if you please to
have the will.[6] Tis enough for one Age to have neglected Mr Cowley, and sterv'd Mr Buttler; but neither
of them had the happiness to live till your Lordship's
Ministry. In the meane time be pleasd to give me a
gracious and speedy answer to my present request of
halfe a yeares pention for my necessityes. I am goeing
to write somewhat by his Majestyes command,[7] & cannot stirr into the Country for my health and studies,
till I secure my family from want. You have many petitions of this nature, & cannot satisfy all, but I hope

from your goodness to be made an Exception to your*a*
generall rules; because I am, with all sincerity,

Your Lordship's most obedient

Humble Servant

John Dryden.

Letter 11

DRYDEN TO JACOB TONSON

Monday Morn:

Mr Tonson

　　The two Melons you sent I receivd before your
letter, which came foure houres*a* after: I tasted one of
them, which was too good to need an excuse; the other
is yet untouchd. You have written diverse things which
gave me great satisfaction; particularly that the History
of the League is commended: & I hope the onely thing
I feard in it, is not found out. Take it all together, &
I dare say without vanity 'tis the best translation of any
History in English, though I cannot say 'tis the best
History; but that is no fault of mine. I am glad my
Lord Duke of Ormond has one: I did not forget him;
but I thought his sorrows were too fresh upon him, to
receive*b* a present of that nature.[1] For my Lord Roscomons Essay, I am of your opinion, that you shou'd
reprint it, & that you may safely venture on a thousand

---

a your *written between the lines*

---

a houres *written between the lines*

b receive *written above an illegible word, which is lined through*

more.[2] in my verses before it, pray let the printer mend
his errour, & let the line stand thus, That heer his Con-
que'ring Ancestors were nursd:—Charles his copy is all
true.[3] The other faults my Lord Roscomon will mend
in the booke, or Mr Chetwood[4] for him, if my Lord be
gone for Ireland: of which, pray send me word. Your
opinion of the Miscellanyes is likewise mine: I will for
once lay by the Religio Laici, till another time.[5] But I
must also add, that since we are to have nothing but
new, I am resolvd we will have nothing but good,
whomever we disoblige. You will have of mine four
Odes of Horace, which I have already translated, another small translation of forty lines from Lucretius:
the whole story of Nisus & Eurialus, both in the fifth,
& the ninth of Virgils Eneids; & I care not who trans-
lates them beside me, for let him be friend or foe, I
will please my self, & not give off in consideration of
any man. there will be forty lines more of Virgil in another place; to answer those of Lucretius; I meane
those very lines which Montaign has compar'd in those
two poets: & Homer shall sleep on for me: I will not
now meddle with him.[6] and for the Act wch remaines
of the opera,[7] I believe I shall have no leysure to mind
it after I have done what I proposd: for my business
heere is to unweary my selfe, after my studyes, not to
drudge: I am very glad you have payd Mr Jones,[8] because he has carryd him selfe so gentlemanlike to me.
& if ever it lyes in my power I will requite it. I desire to
know whether the Dukes house are makeing cloaths &
putting things in a readiness for the singing opera,[9] to
be playd immediately after Michaelmasse: for the Ac-

tors in the two plays,[10] which are to be acted of mine,
this winter, I had spoken with Mr Betterton by chance
at the Coffee house the afternoon before I came away:
& I believe that the persons were all agreed on, to be
just the same you mentiond. Only Octavia was to be
Mrs Buttler,[11] in case Mrs Cooke[12] were not on the
Stage. And I know not whether Mrs Percivall[13] who
is a Comedian, will do so well for Benzayda. I came
hether for health, & had a kind of Hectique feavour
for a fortnight of the time: I am now much better.
poore Jack[14] is not yet recoverd of an intermitting feavour, of which this is the twelfth day: but he mends, &
now begins to eat flesh: to add to this, my man with
over care of him, is fallen ill too, of the same distemper;
so that I am deep in doctors, 'pothecaryes & Nurses:
but though many in this Country fall sick of feavours,
few or none dye. Your friend Charles continues well.
If you have any extraordinary newes I shoud be glad
to heare it. I will answer Mrs Buttlers letter next week,
for it requires no hast.

I am yours
John Dryden.

Letter 12

WALSH TO DRYDEN

To Mr. Dryden

I confess Sir I have great occasion to make apologies y^t trouble you in this kind without having the honour of being known to you or owning myself. However I trust y^r goodness will pardon it, since 'tis ye opinion of Y^{or} Judgment y^t Causes you the trouble, and the little opinion of my own y^t makes me conceal my self. I can only assure you, y^t I have not so little, as to think I ought to set any great value upon these Compositions;[1] the faults are too palpable even to my self, and as they must appear much plainer to so good a Judge as you are. So deal frankly with me Sir & let me know without any complement your real thoughts of 'em in which I can assure you, you will very much oblidge

        Sr

           Your

             [W. Walsh]

Letter 13

DRYDEN TO ETHEREGE

London, Feb. 16th 87 [86/87]

A guilty man, you know S^r naturally avoids one who can convince him of his faults, & I acknowledge myself to be of that number. for which reason I have not dared in three weeks time since your last letter lay by me, yet to open it. for my conscience tells me, that tho' you may express yourself with all imaginable civility, & I believe kindness too, yet there must be somewhat of upbraiding me for my neglect, which I will not go about to excuse, because I cañot. 'tis a blott, and you may enter, if you will. not forgive an oversight, wch you may safely do & win the game afterwards in good writing. for I will never enter the lists in Prose with the undoubted best Author of it wch our nation has produc'd. Therefore O thou iṁortal source of Idleness (you see I am ready to make prayers to you, and invoke you by your darling attribute, pardon a poor creature who is your image, & whom no gratitude, no consideration of friendship no letters tho' never so elegantly written can oblige to take up the penn, tho' it be to manage it half an hour. for while I am writing this, I have layd it down and almost concluded with an imperfect sentence I am almost lazy enough to get a Stamp for my name like the King of France wch indeed wou'd be to be great in idleness—I have made my Court to the King once in seaven moneths, have seen my Lord Chamberlain full as often.[1] I believe if they think of me at all, they imagine I am very proud but

I am gloriously lazy. I have a sonn whom I love intirely, with my Lord Middleton[2] but I never thank him
for his kindness for fear of opening my mouth. I
might probably get something at Court, but my Lord
Sunderland[3] I imagine thinks me dead while I am
silently wishing him all prosperity. for wishes cost me
no more than thinking. In short without Apoplexy,
Wycherleys long sickness[4] I forget every thing to enjoy nothing that is myself. can you expect news out[a]
of Covent Garden from such a man? The Coffee-house[5]
stands certainly where it did, & angry men meet in the
Square sometimes, as Abercomy, and Goodman lately
did. where they say Alexander the Great[6] was wounded
in the arme. by which you may note, he had better have
been idle. I cannot help hearing, that white Sticks[7]
change their Masters, & y[t] officers of y[e] Army are not
immortall in their places because the King finds they
will not vote for him in the next Sessions. Oh that our
Monarch wou'd encourage noble idleness by his own
example, as he of blessed memory did before him for
my minde misgives me, that he will not much advance
his affaires by Stirring[8] I was going on but am glad to
be admonish'd by the paper. ask me not of Love. for
every man hates every man perfectly, & women are
still the same Bitches. but after all I will contradict
myself and come off with an exception as to my own
particular, who am as much as idleness will dispence
with me. S[r.] Your most faithfull Servant

John Dryden.

---

[a] out *written above* from, *which is lined through*

Letter 14

ETHEREGE TO DRYDEN

Ratisbonne 10/20 March. 1686/7

Sr. (Mr. Dreyden)

You know I am no flatterer, & therefore you
will excuse me, when I tell you, I cannot endure you
shou'd arrogate a thing to yourself you have not the
least pretence to. is it not enough that you excelle in
so many eminent vertues, but you must be a putting in
for a Vice which all the world knows is properly my
province. if you persist in your Claim to laziness, you
will be thought as affected in it as Montaigne is, when
he complains of the want of memory. what Soul has
ever been more active than your own? what countrey
nay what corner of the earth has it not travaill'd into?
whose bosom has it not div'd into, [&] inform'd it self
so perfectly of all the Secrets of mans heart that onely
the great being (whose image it bears) knows them
better? I (whose every action of *my* life is a witness of
my idleness) little thought yt you, who have rais'd so
many immortall monuments of your industry durst
have set up to be my Rival. but to punish you I will
distinguish. you have noe share in that noble Laziness
of minde, wch. all I write make[s] out my just title to;
but as for that of the body. I can let you come in for a
Snack without any jealousy. I am apt to think you
have bated something of your mettle since you and I
were Rivalls in other matters tho' I hope you have not
yet obtain'd the perfection I have hear'd Sr Charles

Sidley brag of, wch. is, that when a short youth runs quick through every veine, & puts him in minde of his ancient prowess, he thinks it not worth while to bestow motion on his *et caetera muscle.* Tho' I have not been able formerly to forbear playing the fool in verse and prose I have now judgement enough to know how much I ventur'd, & am rather amaz'd at my good fortune, than vain upon a little success, & did I not see my own error, the commendation you give me wou'd be enough to perswade me of it. a woman who has luckily been thought agreeable, has not reason to be proud, when she hears herself^a extravagantly prais'd by an un-doubted beauty. it wou'd be a pretty thing for a man, who has learn'd of his own head to scrape on the fiddle to enter the list with the greatest Master in the science of musick—it is not to contend with you in writing but to view with you in kindness, that makes me fond of your Correspondence. & I hope my want of Art in friendship will make you forgett the faults it makes me commit in writing. I have not time now to acquaint you, how I like my employment. nature no more in-tended me for a Polititian than she did you for a Cour-tier.[1] but since I am imbarck'd I will endeavour not to be wanting in my duty. it concerns me nearly for shou'd I be shipwreck'd the season is too far gone to expect an other adventure. the conversation I have with the ministers here improves me dayly more in Philosophie, than in Policy. & shews me, that the most necessary part of it is better to be learn'd in the wide

^a prais'd *lined through after* herself

world, than in the gardens of Epicurus. I am glad to hear your son is in the office, hoping now & then by your favour to have the benefit of a letter from him. Pray tell S^r. Henry Shere. his honesty and good understanding have made me Love him Ever since I knew him. if we meet in England again, he may find the gravity of this place has fitted me for his Spanish humour² I was so pleas'd with reading your letter y^t I was vexd at the last proof you gave me of your Laziness. the not finding it in your heart to turn over the paper. In that you have had the better of me, but I will always renounce that darling sin, rather than omit any thing which may give you an assurance of my being faithfully &c

Letter 15

DRYDEN TO WALSH

My Dear Padron

Nothing cou'd please me better, than to know you as well by the endowments of your Mind, as by^a those of your person. I knew before this discovery, that you were ingenious, but not that you were a Poet, & one of the best that these times produce, or the Succeeding times can expect. Give me leave not onely to honour, but to Love you; and I shall endeavour on

---

^a by *written between the lines*

my part, to make more advances to you, than you have
made to me, who am both by gratitude & by inclination
               Your most faithfull humble Servant
                    John Dryden.
   For My Honourd Friend
   William Walsh. Esq
   These.

                    Letter 16

                 WALSH TO DRYDEN

   Dear Sir
      You will see how easy 'tis to encourage an ill
Writer into yᵉ troubling you. The favourable opinion
you shewd of yᵉ songs: have made mee send you an
Epigram & an Elegy, which I fancy to bee better in
their kinds than yᵉ songs, because they are kinds yᵗ I
think I unde[rstand] better. An Epigram 'tis true is
but a Trifle, but so d[iffi]cult a Trifle yᵗ Rapin says 'tis
enough to have ma[de] one good in ones Life time;[1]
I remember you said when wee talkt about these things
at yᵉ Coffee house, yᵗ there were not above 20 good
Epigrams in Martial & I'll undertake wⁿ you have
chose those 20 to make some reasonable objection agt
one half of 'em,[a] particularly in yᵗ wᶜʰ you say is yᵉ
best of yᵉ Book,[2] & truly I am of yʳ Opinion. In yᵉ
first verse to have made it exact, hee ought not[b] to have

   [a] which *lined through immediately after* 'em
   [b] not *written between the lines*

named ye Eunuch Dindymus, except hee had named ye Old man too; but because this is rather a want of Perfection yⁿ a Fault; you may observe in ye 3^d. Verse Viribus hic operi non est, hic utilis annis. The Poet has unfounded his own sense, for hee means y^t this is not useful upon ye account of his want of strenght, & this for his too many years. Which hee expresses only this is not useful upon account of his strenght, this of his years, as if too little was to bee supplyd in one place, & too many in ye other out of ye Readers Invention. I dont say this as if I pretended my own Epigram was comparable to any of his, but to show y^{tc} a thing may bee very beautiful [& y]et have some blemish. The Elegy³ is upon ye same [subj]ect wth ye 11 El: of ye 3^d Book of Ovid; which beeing [e]steemd ye best^d of all his, is disadvantage enough to any [bod]y y^t is to write upon it afterwards. I shoud not trouble [you] with these little things, but y^t I have sent you a Discourse I have writt about Women;⁴ which I woud beg you at yor leisure to look over & tell mee your opinion of it; as also of ye Verses. I see my self 'tis incorrect, but twas writt in haste, in obedience to the command of a fair Lady. Tis not Ill assure you Sir out of any want of respect, if I have not made you all the advances imaginable, as you pleasd to tell mee in yor Letters; But methinks I am ashamed to profess y^t in words y^t I am not able to perform in actions, But I'll assure you, if there were any thing in which I were capable of serv-

c y^e *lined through immediately after* y^t
d y^e best *written between the lines*

ing you, you shoud finde y^t no man in y^e World were
with more zeal then my self.

Dear Sir

Yo^r most Affectionate ffriend
& most Humble Serv$^{t.}$

Letter 17

DRYDEN TO WALSH

You command me Deare Sir, to make a kind of
critique on your Essay: 'tis an hard province; but if I
were able to undertake it, possibly, a greater proofe of
friendship is scarcely to be found; where to be truly a
friend, a man must seeme to exercise a little malice. As
it happens, I am now incumberd with some necessary
business, relating to one of my Sonns; which when it is
over, I shall have more leysure to obey you, in case
there appeare any farther need. There is not the least
occasion of reflecting on your disposition of the piece,
nor the thoughts. I see nothing to censure in either of
them. Besides this the style is easy and naturall; as fit
for Dialogue, as if you had set Tully before you; and
as gallant as Fontenelle in his plurality of Worlds.[1]
In the correctness of the English there is not much for
me to animadvert. Be pleasd therefore, to avoid the
words, don't, can't, shan't, and the like abbreviations of
syllables; which seem to me to savour of a little rus-

ticity. As for Pedantry you are not to be taxd with it.
I remember I hinted somewhat of concludding your
Sentences with prepositions or conjunctions sometimes,
which is not elegant, as in your first sentence—(See the
consequences of). I find likewise, that you make not a
due distinction betwixt that, and who; a man *that* is not
proper; the relative *who* is proper. *That,* ought alwayes to signify a thing; *who,* a person. An acquaint-
tance *that* wou'd have *undertook* the business; true
English is, an acquaintance who wou'd have *undertaken*
the business. I am confident I need not proceed with
these little criticisms, which are rather cavillings.
Philareque,[2] or the Critique on Balzac, observes it as
a fault in his style, that he has in many places written
twenty words together (en suitte) which were all
Monosyllables. I observe this in some lines of your
Noble Epigramm: and am often guilty of it myselfe
through hastinesse. Mr. Waller counted this a vertue
of the English tongue, that it cou'd bring so many
words of the Teutonique together, and yet the smooth-
ness of the Verse not vitiated. Now I am speaking of
your Epigramm,[3] I am sure you will not be offended
with me for saying, there is some imperfection in the
two last lines.

Blend 'em together, Fate, ease both theire paine;
And of two wretches make one happy man. The word
blend includes the sense of *together;* ease both their
paine: paine is Singular, both is Plurall. But indeed
paine may have a collective and plurall signification.
Then the Rhyme is not full of pain and Man. An half

rhyme is not always a fault; but in the close of any paper of verses, tis to be avoyded. And after all, tell me truly, if those words, ease both their paine; were not superfluous in the sence, and onily put, for the sake of the rhyme, and filling up the verse. It came into my head to alter them, and I am affrayd for the worse.

Kind Fate, or Fortune, blend them, if you can: And, of two wretches, make one happy man. Kind fate looks a little harsh: fate without an epithet, is always taken in the ill sence. *Kind* added, changes that signification. (Fati valet hora benigni.) The words (if you can) have almost the same fault I tax'd in your ending of the line: but being better considerd, that is, whether fortune or fate, can alter a Man's temper, who is already so temperd: and leaving it doubtfull, I thinke does not prejudice the thought, in the last line. Now I begin, to be in for Cakes and Ale; and why should I not put a quere on those other lines? Poor Shift, does all his whole contrivance set, To spend that wealth he wants the Sence to get. All his whole Contrivance, is but all his Contrivance, or his whole Contrivance; thus, one of those words, lookes a little like tautology.[4] Then an ill natur'd man might ask, how he cou'd spend wealth, not having the sence to get it? But this is trifling, in me. For your sence is very intelligible; which is enough to secure it. And, by your favour, so is Martial's: Viribus hic non est, hic non est utilis annis: and yet in exactness of Criticism, your censure stands good upon him.—[5] I am call'd to dinner, and have onily time to add a great truth; that I am from the bottome of my Soul, Deare Sir, Your most humble Servant and true lover

John Dryden.

Your apostrophe's to your Mistresse, where you break off the thrid of your discourse, and address youreself to her, are, in my opinion, as fine turnes of gallantry, as I have mett with anywhere.[6]

For my Honour'd Friend,
William Walsh Esqr.
These.

Letter 18

WALSH TO DRYDEN

I give you infinite thanks, Dear Sir, for ye trouble you have given yor self in yor Criticism. To tell any body of y^r fault wth a design y^t they shoud mend 'em, is certainly ye highest art of friendship; To tell 'em y^t others may avoid 'em, is an just end of criticising; But to do 'em only, to lessen one mans reputation wthout any design of bettering anothers is w^t is properly calld Malice. I shall take care to correct those little faults you finde & w^n you have more leisure shall beg you to look it over again. I saw a great many of ye faults you finde in my Epigram before, & am now very sensible of ye rest. I made y^t very objection ag^t shifts spending Wealth, wth out beeing able to get it, to one y^t I shewd

em to; That a man may spend Wealth wth out knowing
how to get it, wee have instances of several [p]eople
born to good Estates y^t do; but y^n ye Poor shift [go?]es
to take away y^t defence; But however shift [being?] a
sort of Hangeron, may contrive to spend [Weal?]th
for other people, wch yet hee is unable to get again.
[Yt?] was w^t I satisfyd my self wth at ye s^d time [wth?]
out thinking farther upon it; th' truly I question
[ve?]ry much whether twill defend it or no; The *all*
whole I confess I did not reflect upon but however 'tis
very plain seen today. The *ease y^t pain*[1] I was so little
satisfyd wth*^{a}* y^t w^n I writt 'em down first in my [T]able
books I durst not make use of it, for both ye reasons
you mention; y^t it was not a good rhyme & perfectly a
boteling out ye Verse; & tho' I had my choice of several
other endings, yett I first writt it out, & left*^{b}* ye Verse
to bee finishd after, because all ye ways I coud think of
were lyable to ye same objection of boteling up y^e
Verse; Your correction of it is much*^{c}* better y^n any of
mine, yet it seems (at least at first sight) to bee a little
faulty too.

I am

Dear Sir

^{a} wth *written between the lines*
^{b} it wth out *lined through after* left
^{c} much *written between the lines*

Letter 19

WALSH TO DRYDEN

Dear Sir

Wee young Authours are like young Women, who are allways plaguing a Man, when hee is once acquainted wth y^r infirmities. I have lookt over my Dialogue of Women, & if I can judge of my own things, as impartially as of other peoples, I think it^a not much worse yⁿ many other things y^t are printed with tolerable Success. However tis upon a particular reason y^t I woud have it printed; of wch I will make you Confident; The Lady to whom it is written has playd mee some scurvy trickes for which I may come to fall out publickly with her. & because it is usual for all^b ye Sex to take one anothers part in these case[s]; I wou'd first print this Defence of 'em, to engage my self a party amongst 'em,[1] There is another reason also, & y^t is, I have another Mistress, who is resolved to con-ferr favour upon none but Merit; & as shee is a person of sense, so shee does place all this merit, as Women usually do, in a fine outside; But is a great friend to Witt & Learning; If I coud therefore any ways make her believe y^t I had any pretences to those, it might bee a great meens towards ye making mee succeed. The Business therefore is that I have hardly confidence enough in it, to print in my own name; on ye other side shoud it bee printed wthout any name at all, it may per-haps never come to bee read: Now if you woud give yor

---

^a may do *lined through after* it   ^b all *written over* y^e

selfe ye trouble to write some little preface to it, it
might [*sic*] a very great means to recommend it to y^e
World. Tis true I am no great friend to^c Letters of
Recommendation before Books nor I believe does any
of solid Judgem^t ever like 'em ye better for it, but this
beeing intended only for ye Ladies, ye know they are
often imposed upon by such things. It is a very usual
thing amongst ye French, for one friend to write prefaces for another; however I do not much fancy y^t manner of doing it; wch is a fulsome Panegyrick upon y^e
Work. All y^t I woud have done in the case, is to
acquaint em, y^t ye Author of it having not confidence
enough in ye piece to venture it to ye press; you thought
y^t it might pass as well as others y^t they have been
troubled with. If you finde any thing in ye manner, of
ye Dialogue, in ye Gallantry of ye Apostrophes, or if
you think there is somew^t of reading shewn in it, y^t is
considerable for a man who professes himself so perfect
a serv^t to ye Sex, you may please to let 'em know as
much.[2] I wou'd by no means impose so far upon yor
friendship, as to desire you to say any thing more y^n
w^t you think, but if you think there is any thing tolerable in it, you may let 'em know y^t. All y^t can reason-
ally be urged ag^t this is, y^t I having^d spoken with
Justice of some of yor things in it, y^t may look like a
bribe to you to^e say some thing of mine.[3] But, in answer to this 'tis plain, y^t if I have said more of you y^n
of any other of o^r Contemporaries, tis^f evidently for

^{c} commendate *lined through after* to
^{d} com *lined through after* having
^{e} return ye com *lined through after* to
^{f} only *lined through after* tis

noe other reason but because you deserve it better &
y^t I have every where taken all occasions of mentioning
any Witt of o^r own Times; as a piece of Candour w^{ch}
I have very much admired in some great Authors, &
ye contrary to wch seems only to bee marks of ill Malice. If you^g have leisure,^{h} to do this & dont think y^e
piece unworthy it. I will send you the Copy, wch you
may dispose of with ye same freedom as if it were yor
own, reserving mee^i as sufficient number of Printed
ones to disperse among my friends. I do not mean y^t
you shoud speake of it as a piece of wch ye Author is not
known, for tho' I will not venture to put my Name,
yet except it is known to bee mine, it will not answer y^e
Ends for wch I design'd it.[4]

I am

D

Letter 20

WALSH TO DRYDEN

I sent you a letter y^t day I came out of Town by my
Chairman, wth a Copy of ye Song to Fluvia enclosed in
it, wch I suppose hee deliverd you. I told you there
also y^t it was not impossible but I might trouble you
wth a letter out of ye Countrey. Accordingly S^r ye time

^{g} will do me *lined through after* you
^{h} & do not think *lined through after* leisure
^{i} some *lined through after* mee

is come & you must bear it as patiently as you can. The
business I write to you ab^t, is a design y^t I have had of
a Treatise, wch I woud have yor Opinion of before I set
ab^t it.[1]

The Treatise I design y^n, is of ye Nature of Love: It
shall bee divided into three parts. In the first wee will
speak of ye Nature of Love in general; wee will shew
y^t this general Inclination wch we [call?] Love is y^e
Cause of all ye Vertues & Vices in ye World as it is
placet before good or bad Objects. Wee shall divide it
into Love of y^e [Minde & of the body.]^a Wee will
shew y^t Love is a tendency of ye Minde [to good]^b &
y^t all ye Errony & Vices y^t proceed from Love, is lov-
ing^c ye lesser Good w^n it is accompanyd wth a greater
Evil; not y^t it makes us love ye Evil, but ye Good does
so blinde us, as to make us not take notice of ye Evil.
Wee will shew y^t Amorousness is so far from beeing a
fault y^t it requires all ye Wisdome & Vertue in ye World
to bee truly so. Wee will shew y^t there can bee no happiness but in Love;^{d} But as ye difference of ye Objects
this Love is placet upon may^e make, y^t bad wch is in its
own nature Good, it draws us insensibly into ye 2d part
wch is ye Object of Love. This wee shall make to bee
Beauty as Socrates^f & Plato has done first, & every body
since from him. Wee shall divide Beauty into^g Beauty of

^{a} Minde ... body *is conjectural; manuscript is mutilated at top of f. 56r.*
^{b} to good *is conjectural; manuscript is mutilated at top of f. 56r.*
^{c} good *lined through before* y^e
^{d} y^t ye Joys of Heaven in a *lined through before* But
^{e} may *written between the lines*
^{f} Socrates & *written between the lines after* as
^{g} Corporeal *lined through immediately after* into

ye Body & ye Minde. Corporeal^h Beauty wee shall divide
into Visible & Invisible. Y^e Visible shall be Colour, Proportion, & Air. The Invisible shall bee y^t Sympathy &
Antipathy wch makes us love w^n there is no Beauty y^t
appears. & y^t makes us love one particular Object w^n
other people love others. As ye Loadstone draws Iron &
not Straws &c: we shall divide the Beauty of ye Minde
into^i Intellectual & Moral in reference to ye facultyes of
ye Minde^j ye Understanding & ye Will. Wee [will
shew]^k [y^e?] Connexion there is between these 3
Beautyes in [them. Wee will^l] shew y^t ye Beauty of y^e
Body is a sign of Beauty of ye Mind; wee will shew y^t
ye Errors y^t happen,^{m} proceed either from mistaking
Beauty; taking y^t Beauty y^t is not really so in y^t Creature. as mistaking Manly Beauty in a Woman or Fem-
inine in a Man. Or from doating upon some little
Beauty, w^n there are other Deformityes, y^t are worse
signs[?] & overcome ye other. Or from an utter De-
pravation of o^r Understanding, wch makes it delight in
w^t is not Beautiful.

The third part shall bee of Enjoym^t. Wee will shew
y^t as Love allways tends to Enjoym^t, so will shew w^t it
[proposes?] to it self in it. wch is production of somew^t
Beautiful^n in order to satisfy y^t inbred Desire wee have
of Immortality. That as there are 3 sort of Love so
there are 3 sorts of Ways to do this. ye 1st Corporeal by

^{h} In *lined through before* Corporeal
^{i} y^t of ye Understanding & ye Will *lined through after* into
^{j} Intell *lined through after* Minde
^{k} will shew *written in as catch words at bottom of f. 56r. by another hand*
^{l} *conjectural; manuscript is mutilated at top of f. 56v.*
^{m} is *lined through after comma*
^{n} Beautiful *written between the lines*

Children. ye 2^d Intellectual by wise Discourse Writing
&c: ye 3^d Moral by good & Vertuous Action.^{o} Wee will
shew y^t all Happiness even In ye Happiness of Heaven,
is only enjoying w^t wee love. Wee will take occasion
here to shew why some Loves do nott last after En-
joym^t. Wee will speak here of Marriage, & taking it
for granted y^t they are generally unfortunate, endevour
w^t ye reasons of it.

Now to make it both more^p Instructive, & more entertaining too, I wou'd treat it by way of Dialogue. I
woud lay ye Scene of it in France as beeing a place where
they are apter to talk of Love y^n here. I woud have it
ye Hostel Rambouillet wch was ye rendezvous of all y^e
Beaux Esprits of y^t Age. & I woud bring in La
Chambre, Balzac, & Voiture talking ab^t it. La Chambre^2
because no Man has treated ye Passions so judiciously or
so floridly. Balzac^3 because hee set up Morals to talk
of ye Moral part; & Voiture^4 & ye Ladye^q for ye Gallantry, wch will be necessary to set of ye Piece.

W^t m[ay] bee objected ag^t this is, y^t it is doing too
much honour to another Countrey especially at a time
w^n wee are at War wth 'em;^{5} tho' in answer to y^t I
think 'tis no more to bring 'em in in a Dialogue, y^n to
translate any thing y^t they have written.^{6}

Pray let mee know whether you approve of ye Design or no, & whether you think it bee wth in my
strenght. I have drawn you such a confused Scheme of

---

^{o} Here wee may take occasion to give reasons why Love does not last after
Enjoym^t *lined through after* action

^{p} plain *lined through after* more

^{q} & ye Ladye *written between the lines*

it, y[t] I do not know whether you will take it right, but however you may guess at my design by it.[7]

But I trouble you too long ab a Trifle, & take you of from[r] Employm[t.] y[e] World will bee much more concerned in. Is Cleomenes finisht pray[8] or have you begun y[e] other design you told mee of ab[t] y[e] priesthood.[9]

Pray Let mee know w[n] you go out of Town & whither. Have you heard out of Staff, I had a letter from London w[ch] told mee[s] y[e] young Lady was just going to be marryd to a young L[d] whose name they coud not tell.[10] That is not fair play methinkes to take so considerable place, w[th]out proclaiming War.

Abberley[11]
   August 13: 1691

Letter 21

WALSH TO DRYDEN

S[r]
      I am very sorry to hear you have but [*sic*] been well, but hope the Thunder has cleard y[e] Air, & made it fitter for you tho not perfect for[a] Poetry I see will still bee reserved to y[e] same Destiny & methinks Homer who went wth a Dog & Bell[b] ab[t] alone, had somew[t] y[e] ad-

---

[r] better *lined through after* from
[s] thee *lined through after* mee

---

[a] tho not perfect for *written between the lines*
[b] wth a Dog & Bell *written between the lines*

vantage of*c* a Man y^t goes about in some sort of Mens
Company. But who is ye Lord pray y^t was talkt of for
ye fair Lady for this is ye first y^t*d* you told mee of it.[1]
Since I rec^d yo^rs I have lookt over Castiglione; where
hee treats of Love:[2] Speron Sperone has a Dialogue
upon ye same Occasion:[3] Tassone has some Chapters
ab^t it in his Pensieri,[4] & Alveto d'Equicola has writt a
Book wch hee calls De Natura di Amore.[5] I give you
in his own words, because it is not very good Italian, for
now at least they say della Nature d'Amore. These are
all ye Italians y^t I have seen ab^t it, if therefore y^t you
mention bee any thing else, I shou'd bee glad to see it if I
knew w^t it was: Tho' Truly these woud give me little
encouragem^t, for there is nothing new in em. Le
Chambre[6] is ye only Modern y^t has treated y^t Subject
well, & indeed as a Naturalist he has gone farther in it
y^n any of ye Antients. But ye chief Man I intend to
follow is Plato: who has writt one Dialogue of Love,
& one*e* of Beauty & ye latter indeed altogether allegorical*f* y^t of Love is one of ye best y^t ever hee writt.[7] The
Dialogue consists of a great many, & [so on?] y^t give*g*
accounts of this Passion all severally, & all very entertaining. But as there are but 3 ways of considering it,
one as a Naturalist, one as a Moralist, & one as*h* a Gallant, I made choice of those 3 persons to do it. In y^e
two last of*i* whose Characters I finde you think there is

c Men *lined through after* of
d I heard *lined through after* y^t
e one *written above* 2
f y^e ... allegorical *written between the lines*
g several *lined through after* give
h one as *written between the lines*
i y^e two last of *written between the lines*

a great deal of difficulty.[8] Now y^t of Boileaus by y^e way is quite a different undertaking, for 'tis one thing to^j imitate y$^{t\,k}$ writing, another thing y^t speaking; & hee y^t shoud bring in Cicero^l talking in a Dialogue wth all those long^m & elaborate Periods y^t hee uses in his Orations, wou'd quite destroy y^e Nature of this sort of Writing. Tis true indeed Letters ought to bee y^e way of writing the most like speaking, but as Demetrius Phalereus[9] tells you y^t even in his time they were allowd to bee much more flourishing in one y^n in ye other; So Balzacks Letters are in a Stile much more different from ye common way of talking y^n any in his times. And you see w^n hee writes his Moralls^n as well as his familiar Letters to Conrart & Chapelain,[10] hee leaves all^o those affected Hyperboles & Metaphors, y^t hee commonly made use of, as not proper in y^t place. So now^p y^t my business is n^t I reckon to look upon him as an Orator but a Moral Philosopher. By ye way do you think Boileau has so extremely well succeeded in his Imitation of him. I confess I allways thought it a chef d'Oevre, till looking upon it again after ye receipt of yor letter, it does not appear to mee so well as formerly, & I^q will tell you my reason, y^t you may inform mee better if I am in ye Wrong. Balzac you know was ye first y^t brought ye French Prose to any thing of Excellence. ^{r}No Modern in any language has imitated ye beauty of Ciceros Numbers like him, & there is nothing

---

^{j} represent *lined through after* to
^{l} spe *lined through after* Cicero
^{n} hee *lined through after* Moralls
^{p} now *written between the lines*
^{r} There *lined through after the period*

^{k} y^t *written over* 'em
^{m} Periods *lined through after* long
^{o} y^t *lined through after* all
^{q} may *lined through after* I

more full, more musical, round, more majestical[s] or
more harmonious y[n] his Numbers. his connexion very
fine[t] Hee writes in y[t] Sublime Stile y[t] Longin talks so
much of, & this has[u] sometimes carryd him too far, into
too bold Metaphor & too[v] strong Hyperboles. Now
pray how does Boileau imitate this. His periods are
short, rough, & unmusical no connexion at all between
em more like Seneca or Lipsius[11] y[n] Cicero or Balzac[w];
but to make amends hee has given you three times more
Hyperboles y[n] ever Balzac made use of in y[e] same compass. I confess it puts mee in mind of Kg Charles y[e]
2d Picture upon the sign Posts, where the Painters
thought if they made a damnd ugly face wth a black
Periwigg they had done y[r] businesse. If a man woud
enter into ye retail of these businesses one might make
several Criticismes upon y[t] letter. Le bruit de vos actions ressuscite les morts: Il reveille des gens endormis
depuis trente annees, & condamnes a un[x] sommeil eter-
nel. Il fait parler le silence même. Is[y] not there
enough of y[t] sort for one letter & yet before ye ending of
it, you finde; Il fait sans cesse ressouvenir de vous dans
le sejour mêmes de l'oubli: Il trouve des partizans zeles
dans le pais de l'indifference: If there are ye same sort
of thoughts & numbers[z] these were too many of this
sort to come together as indeed they were, they were
much worse to come upon you again so soon after.[12]

---

[s] round, more majestical *written between the lines*
[t] his connexion very fine *written between the lines*
[u] of *lined through after* has   [v] high *lined through after* too
[w] more . . . Balzac *written between the lines*
[x] silence *lined through after* un   [y] there *lined through after* is
[z] There . . . numbers *written between the lines*

And yet as if hee had done enough in y^t hee brings 'em upon you again in Voitures letter; Il s'est fait entendre dans un lieu ou l'on n'entend pas Dieu tonner, & a fait connaitre votre gloire dans un pays ou l'on ne connaist point le Soleil. This is not ye only ye same thing over again, but it is brought in where it is not near so proper. Not but y^t I confess I look upon his letter in imitation of Voiture as admirably well done. His Character[13] indeed is very hard to hitt; & y^t indeed I take to bee difficulty of ye piece. For his letters are so very natural & easy, y^t nothing can bee more proper for Dialogue. But besides^{aa} beeing very conversant in his Style, a Man must bee in a good hum^r w^n hee woud imitate him or else hee will make nothing of it. I wou'd send you a Copy of some Letters in his way but y^t I have tired you too much allready.

I am
S^r

Letter 22

DRYDEN TO THE EARL OF DORSET

My Lord

A long indisposition of six weeks has hindered me from paying you my acknowlegment for your last favours, and now your poor servant Mr Munson[1] not having the confidence to wait upon you himself has de-

aa understand *lined through after* besides

sired me to sollicit for him with your Lordship for a
favour in which your onely recommendation will make
him happy. If Queen Dowager, as we believe, is going
for Portugal many Lodgings in Summerset house will
be empty, in which case may your Lordship be pleased
to recommend him to my Lord Feversham[2] for a spare
room or two, which will disburden him of halfe the
Charges of his poor subsistence: if I had confidence
enough my Lord, I would presume to mind you of a
favour which your Lordship formerly gave me some
hopes of from the Queen;[3] but if it be not proper or
convenient for you to ask, I dare give your Lordship no
further trouble in it, being on so many other accounts
allready your Lordship's most oblig'd obedient Servant

John Dryden.

Octob: 7th.
Thursday

Letter 23

TONSON TO DRYDEN

Sir,
    I have here returned ye Ovid, wch I read wth a
great deal of pleasure, & think nothing can be more entertaining; but by this letter you find I am not soe well
satisfied as perhaps you might think. I hope at ye same
time the matter of fact I lay down in this letter will

appear grounds for it, & wch I beg you woud concider of; & then I believe I shall at least bee excused.

You may please S^r to remember that upon my first proposal about ye 3^d Missellany,[1] I offerd fifty pounds & talkd of several Authours without naming Ovid; You ask'd if it shou'd not be guynneas, & said I shoud not repent it; upon wch I imediately complyd, & left it wholy to you what, & for ye quantity too: and I declare it was the farthest in ye world from my thoughts that by leaving to you I shoud have the less. Thus the case stood, when you went into Essex. After I came out of Northamptonshire I wrote to you, and reseived a Letter dated monday Oct. 3^d. 92. from wch letter I now write word for word what followes:

"I am translating about six hundred lines, or somewhat less, of ye first book of the Metamorphoses. If I cannot get my price, wch shall be twenty guynneas, I will translate the whole book; wch coming out before the whole translation will spoyl Tate's undertakings.[2] 'Tis one of the best I have ever made, and very pleasant. This, wth Heroe & Leander, & the piece of Homer, (or, if it be not enough, I will add more) will make a good part of a Missellany."[3]

Those S^r are ye very words, & ye onely ones in that letter relating to that affair. & ye monday following you came to town.— After your arrivall you shew'd Mr. Motteaux[4] what you had done wch he told me was ye end of ye Story of Daphnis, & demanded as you mentiond in your letter, twenty guyneas, wch that Bookseller refusd. Now, S^r I the rather believe there was just soe much done, by reason ye number of lines you mention in yor letter agrees wth ye quantity of lines that soe much of ye first book makes; wch upon counting ye Ovid I find to be in ye lattin 566, in ye English 759; & ye Bookseller told me there was noe more demanded of him for it.— Now S^r what I entreat you wou'd please to consider of is this: that it is reasonable for me to expect at least as much favour from you as a strange Bookseller; and I will never believe y^t it can be in yor nature to use one ye worse for leaveing it to you; & if the matter of fact as I state it be true, (& upon my word what I mention I can shew you in yor letter,) then pray S^r consider how much dearer I pay then you offered it to ye other Bookseller; for he might have had to ye end of ye Story of Daphnis for 20 guynneas, wch is in yor translation . . . .   759 lines; & then suppose 20 guyneas more for

the same number. . . . .   759 lines, that makes for 40 guyneas . . . .   1518 lines; And all that I have for fifty guyneas are but 1446; soe that if I have noe more, I pay 10 guynneas above 40, & have 72 lines less for fifty, in proportion, than the other Bookseller shoud have had for 40, at ye rate you offered him ye ffirst part. This is, Sir, what I shall take as a great favour if you please to think of. I had intentions of letting you know this before; but till I had paid ye money I would not ask to see ye book, *nor count the lines,* least it shoud look like a design of not keeping my word.[5] When you have looked over ye rest of what you have already translated, I desire you would send it; & I own y^t if you dont think fit to ad something more, I must submit: 'tis wholy at yor choice, for I left it intirely to you; but I believe you cannot imagine I expected soe little; for you were pleased to use me much kindlyer in Juvenall[6] wch is not reckond soe easy to translate as Ovid. *S^r, I humbly beg yor pardon for this long letter, & upon my word I had rather have y^r good will than any* mans alive; &, whatever you are pleasd to doe will alway acknowledge my self S^r

Yo^r most obliged humble Servt,
J. Tonson.

Letter 24

DRYDEN TO WALSH

You may well wonder my Friend, that I have not written to you in so long a time, when I have nothing but laziness to plead in my excuse; which is not, nor ought to be a reasonable plea. Yet I cou'd offer another reason for not writeing; if my letters were worth excuseing. I am up to the Eares in law; & have been for six weekes together. I have been cousend of fifty pounds, & more, by one whom I thought my Friend: & am affrayd that at the long run, I will rather loose it, & let him go, whom I have arrested, than prosecute him in the tedious court of Chancery; to do which I must pass through a tedious course of Common Law.[1] But to leave this, there passes nothing in the Town worth your knowing. Durfey has brought another farce upon the Stage: but his luck has left him: it was sufferd but foure dayes; and then kickd off for ever.[2] Yet his Second Act, was wonderfully diverting; where the scene was in Bedlam: & Mrs Bracegirdle and Solon were both mad: the Singing was wonderfully good, And the two whom I nam'd, sung better than Redding[3] and Mrs Ayloff,[4] whose trade it was: at least our partiality carryed it for them. The rest was woefull stuff, & concluded with Catcalls; of which the two noble Dukes of Richmond[5] and St Albans[6] were chief managers. For other newes 'tis all uncertain. But we all believe that the King of France, who was to set out from Versailles, on Saturday last, is gone for Flanders; & intends to offer Battle: in order to wch we thinke he will besiege Maestrickt: the country about wch being plaine & open, He may^a poure in his horse upon them; of wch he has fifty thousand, & the Confederates not above half that number. The great Turke takes the field this yeare in person; as our foreign Gazettes tell us. As for our descent on France; either we never did intend it; or we do still: & I believe the latter. For without prejudice or partiality, I look upon the Confederacy to be upon its last legg after this Campaign, if K: William does not attempt something very extraordinary, & succeed in it.[7] For which reason, I thinke you are very much in the right, not to press into publique business, till you see the success of this ensueing Summer.[8] I spoke with a Young Gentleman, who is just arrivd from Flanders & came from Bruxelles. He assures me, that not above a fortnight ago, the French burnt a village, within a

^a may *written twice*

mile of the Town; & the Garrison, though they knew
of it, yet durst not ventureout. that the Town wishes
the French were Masters of it; & that generally the
Hollanders are desirous of a peace. This is still to con-
firme you in your opinion of sitting still. I spoke to
Mr Tonson to send you down the Bookes you down the
Bookes [*sic*] you desir'd; in order to the writeing of a
preface before my next Play: if he has not done it, I
will remind him of it. For I shall be very proud, of
your entring into the lists, though not against Rymer;
yet as a champion for our cause, who defy the Chorus
of the Ancients.[9] The play I am now writeing is a
feignd story: & a Tragicomedy of the nature of the
Spanish Fryar: And I am sure the tale of it is likely to
be diverting enough. I have plotted it all; & written
two Acts of it. This morning I had their chief Comedian whom they call Solon,[10] with me; to consult with
him concerning his own Character: & truly I thinke he
has the best Understanding of any man in the Play-
house. Mr Wycherleys Poems will not come out, till
Michaelmass terme: if his versification prove as [well?]
as his wit, I shall believe it will be extraordinary. However Congreve & Southern[11] & I, shall not faile to appeare before it. & if you will come in, he will have
reason to acknowledge it for a favour.[12] And, on our
sides, you shall be very welcome to make up the
[Mass?]. I had this day a letter from my Sonns at
Rome;[13] which to my wonder tells me, that on our fif-
teenth of Aprill (on which they dated) they were in
the extreamity of hott weather: so that they cou'd onely

stirr out, morning & evening: & were already in the
midst of peas and cherryes: tis quite*b* contrary heere;
where we have nothing but raine, cold weather, & a
late Spring time, without hope of any Summer. Write
me word if you please, when we may hope to see you
in Town; or whether at all this Summer: & what is
become of the insurrection at Worcester, concerning the
transportation of Corne.[14] You may see*c* I set not up
for a Wit in this letter: Nor will at any time, with you
to whom I profess an entire friendship. I had your
Sydar safe; & it was as perfectly good, as I am sure you
designd it. I am Sir

        Your most faithfull Humble Servant
            John Dryden

Tuesday Afternoon
    May the 9th or 10th

Ffor William Walsh Esqr.
Att Abberley neare Worcester
These.
To be left with the Postmaster of Worcester,
to be conveyd as above directed.
[Mr Dryden Letter]*d*

---

b A blot on the manuscript partially obscures the word, but I read quite
c see *written between the lines*   *d Added in another hand*

Letter 25

DRYDEN TO WALSH

My Friend

Yesterday morning my Lord Leycester sent his Gentleman to me, to let you know by me, that he had made enquiry about the place you mentioned; & found that some dayes before your letter came, it had been given away to one Mr Carey, who had possest it in the time of K: Charles the 2d. and that this Gentleman was actually sworn into it. I suppose that you imagind the place of that benefit, being now worth 1500th y annum, wou'd not be long voyd: & therefore set not your heart upon it.[1] I spoke for places in the coach too late; there will be none voyd till next weeke.[2] Tonson has likewise fayld me in the publishing his Miscellaɲyes.[3] Tho that shou'd not have hinderd me any longer [than?] till Saturday. I thinke I gave you an account of all things in your letter: onely forgot, perhaps, one thing: wch is you desird to know what kind of Book^a it was y^{tb} Hen Herringman or his man publishd under the name of Miscellany-Poems:[4] they are almost all old, as I am informd; & have been most of them printed before. One or two of My Lord Roscomons excepted. No body vallues them; nor woud you, yourselfe, as my Friends tell me. I gave your service to Congreve; who is since gone out of Town for a moneth or six weekes. No newes, I thinke: that of the Ships is at a stand. We

^{a} Book *written above* thing[?], *which is lined through*
^{b} *Indistinct in manuscript, but I read* y^t

have lost about forty or fifty; including the Dutch Merchants: de Tourvilles letter to his King*c* sayes he has destroyd Seaven Dutch & English men of warr; & that he is still in pursuit of merchants ships. Huy, I thinke I told you is taken; & so is Darmstead neere Francfort: the Dauphin & Lorge are gone to find Louis of Baden, who is not above 24 thousand strong: Saxony will not joine him, unless he may command: & in probability, has taken French money, to lye still. The Confederacy totters; for the Emperour is inclind to treat; but France will grant no Cessation in the meane time. All things favour the Monarch, who pushes round him: & our Fleet yesterday was in Torbay: no newes of Rook[5] since his last letter we ghess him gone for Ireland, with the remainder of his scatterd covey.

I am Sir,

Your most Faithfull Servant

John Dryden.

Thursday

For William Walsh Esq
Att Abberley neere Worcester
These.
To be left at the posthouse in
Worcester, & thence conveyd.

---

c to his **King** *written between the lines*

Letter 26

DRYDEN TO TONSON

Mr. Tonson

I am ashamd of my self, that I am so much behind hand with you in kindness. above all things I am
sensible of your good nature, in bearing [me]ᵃ company to this place;¹ wherein besides the cost, you must
needs neglect your own business; but I will endeavour
to make you some amends; & therefore I desire you to
command me something for your service. I am sure
you thought My Lord Radclyffe wou'd have done
something:² I ghessd more truly, that he cou'd not; but
I was too farr ingagd to desist; though I was tempted
to it, by the melancholique prospect I had of it. I have
translated six hunderd lines of Ovid; but I believe I
shall not compasse his 772 lines under nine hunderd or
more of mine. This time I cannot write my wife, because he who is to carry my letter to Oundle, will not
stay till I can write another. Pray' Sir let her know that
I am well; & for feare the few Damsins shoud be all
gone, desire her to buy me a Sieve full, to preserve
whole, & not in Mash. I intend to come up at least a
week before Michaelmass; for Sir Matthew is gone
abroad, I suspect a wooeing and his Caleche is gone
with him: so that I have been but thrice at Tichmarsh,
of which you were with me once. This dissappointment
makes the place wearysome to me, wᶜʰ otherwise woud
be pleasant. About a fortnight ago I had an intimation

ᵃ *a break in the manuscript*

from a friend by letter, That one of the Secretaryes, I suppose Trenchard had informd the Queen, that I had abusd her Government, (those were the words) in my Epistle to my Lord Radclyffe;³ & that thereupon, she had commanded her Historiographer Rymer, to fall upon my Playes; wᶜʰ he assures me is now doeing. I doubt not his malice, from a former hint you gave me: & if he be employd, I am confident tis of his own seeking; who you know has spoken slightly of me in his last Critique: & that gave me occasion to snarl againe.⁴ In your next, let me know what you can learn of this matter. I am Mr Congreve's true Lover & desire you to tell him, how kindly I take his often Remembrances of me: I wish him all prosperity; & hope I shall never loose his Affection. Nor yours Sir; as being Your most Faithfull, & much obligd Servant

John Dryden.

I had all your Letters.

Aug 30.th

> Sir Matthew had your Book, when he came home last; & desird me, to give you his Acknowledgments.

Letter 27

DRYDEN TO TONSON

My Good Friend

This is onely to acquaint you, that I have taken my place in the Oundle Coach for Tuesday next; & hope to be at London on Wednesday night. I had not confidence enough to hope Mr Southern & Mr Congreve woud have given me the favour of their company for the last foure miles; but since they will be so kind to a friend of theirs, who so truely loves both them & you, I will please my self with expecting it if the weather be not so*a* bad, as to hinder them. I assure you I lay up your last kindnesses to me in my heart; & the less I say of them, I charge them to account so much the more; being very sensible that I have not hetherto deservd them. Haveing been obligd to sit up all last night almost, out of civility to strangers, who were benighted & to resign my bed to them, I am sleepy all this day: & If I had not taken a very lusty pike that day, they must have gone supperless to bed, foure Ladyes and two Gentlemen; For Mr Dudley & I were alone with but one Man, & no Mayd in the House This time I cannot write to my wife; do me the favour to let her know I receivd her letter, am well; & hope to be with

_____
a so *written between the lines*

her on Wednesday next at Night. No more; but that
I am Very much

Your Friend & Servant

John Dryden

Wednesday the 13th. of 7ber

For Mr Jacob Tonson
Bookseller, att the Sign of
The Judges Head in Chancery-Lane,
neare Fleetstreet
These
London.

Letter 28

DRYDEN TO WALSH

Deare Mr Walsh

    I have read over your letter many times: & you
know that when we repeat actions often, tis with pleasure. The Method which you have taken, is wonderfully good; & not onely all present Poets, but all who
are to come in England, will thanke you for freeing
them from the too servile imitation of the Ancients.
If heerafter the Audience, will come to tast the confine-
ment of the French (which I believe the English never
will,) then it will be easy for their Poets, to follow the
strictness of the Mechanique rules, in the three Unities.
In the meane time, I am affrayd, for my sake, you dis-

cover not your Opinion, concerning my Irregular way,
of Tragicomedies, in my doppia favola. I beseech you
let no consideration of mine hinder you from makeing
a perfect Critique. I will never defend that practice:
for I know it distracts the Hearers. But I know, with-
all, that it has hitherto pleasd them, for the sake of
variety; & for the particular tast, which they have to
low Comedy. Mascardi, in some of his Miscellany
Treatises, has a Chapter concerning this; & exempli-
fies, in the Satyr & Corisca, of the Pastor Fido:[1] As I
remember those two persons though not of a piece with
the rest, yet serve in the Conclusion, to the discovery
& beauty of the Design. Your Critique, by your description of its bulk, will be to large for a preface to my
Play, which is now studying; but cannot be acted till
after Christmasse is over.[2] I call it Love Triumphant;
or Nature will prevaile: Unless instead of the second
Title, you like this other Neither Side to blame: which
is very proper, to the two chief Characters of the Heroe
& Heroine: who notwithstanding the Extravange [*sic*]
of their passion, are neither of them faulty, either in
duty, or in Honour. Your Judgment of it, if you
please. When you do me the favour to send your
Booke,[3] I will take care to correct the press; & to have
it printed well. It will be more for your Honour, too,
to print it alone, & take off the suspition of your being
too much my friend, I meane too partiall to me, if
it comes in company of my Play. I have rememberd
you to all your friends; and in particular to Congreve;
who sends you his play,[4] as a present from him selfe,
by this conveyance; & much desires the honour of being

better known to you. His Double Dealer is much censurd by the greater part of the Town: and is defended
onely by the best Judges, who, you know, are commonly
the fewest. Yet it gets ground daily, and has already
been acted Eight times. The women thinke he has ex-
posd their Bitchery too much; & the Gentlemen, are
offended with him; *a* for the discovery of their follyes:
& the way of their Intrigues, under the notion of
Friendship to their Ladyes Husbands. My verses,
which you will find before it, were written before the
play was acted. but I neither alterd them nor do I
alter my opinion of the play. For other newes, you will
heare from all hands; that the House of Lords grow
very warm; & have a mind to try the Land Admiralls:
those of the Sea having been acquitted by the Commons: Yet they have orderd Rook,[5] Killigrew, Shovell,
& the Turkesh Merchants, to appeare before them: and
on the other side, the King has taken away the Commiss-
ions of the Marine Admiralls. You know Russell will
be the Man.[6] The Whig party, who brought in the
King, thinke Killigrew & his Brethren Jacobites, & My
Lord Carmarthen[7] with all the High Church men to
be betrayers of the Government. In my Conscience they
wrong them. The Commons are inspecting their own
House, for the private pensions: which Squib[8] pretends
to discover, & will name above an Hunderd men: it
will all come to nothing I believe, by the over votes of
the other side, in both Houses: when they are tir'd,
they will give the Six millions; & next Michaelmass,
we shall have a new Parliament: but for the Trienniall

a them *lined through immediately after* with

Bill, now sent down from the Lords, I conceive it will be thrown out by the Commons: because of the Rider, which explaines the word Holden; not to signify to hold. We heare of about ten of our Easterland Ships & two small Men of Warr, are taken by Du Bart,[9] & carryed into France: they were laden, with corne & other provisions. Last, for my selfe: I have undertaken to translate all Virgil:[10] & as an Essay, have already paraphrasd, the third Georgique, as an Example; it will be publishd in Tonsons next Miscellanyes, in Hillary terme.[11] I propose to do it by subscription; haveing an hunderd & two Brass Cutts, with the Coats of Armes of the Subscriber to each Cutt: & every Subscriber to pay five guinneys: half in hande besides another inferiour Subscription of two Guinneys, for the rest whose names are onely written in a Catalogue, printed with the Book.

I am Dear Sir,
Your most faithfull Servant. John Dryden.
Dec. 12th

I have just receivd your verses to Mr Wycherley: but cannot stay to read them before I put up this letter, 'tis so late att night.[12]

For William Walsh Esq
Att Abberley, neare Worcester
These:
By Worcester Stage Coach.
With a small parcell in
paper, directed to Mr Walsh.

Letter 29

JOHN DENNIS TO DRYDEN

Sir,

Thô no Man writes to his Friends with greater Ease, or with more Chearfulness, than my self; and thô I have lately had the Presumption to place you at the Head of that small Party, nevertheless I have experienc'd Grief, that in writing to you I have not found my old Facility.

Since I came to this place I have taken up my Pen several times in order to write you, but have constantly at the very Beginning found myself Damp'd and Disabled; upon which I have been apt to believe that extraordinary Esteem may sometimes make the Mind as Impotent as Violent Love does the Body, and that the vehement Desire we have to exert it extremely decays our Ability. I have heard of more than one lusty Gallant, who, thô he could at any time with Readiness and Vigour possess the Woman whom he lov'd but moderately, yet when he has been about to give his darling Mistress, whom he has vehemently and long desir'd, the first last Proof of his Passion, has found on a sudden that his Body has Jaded and Grown resty under his Soul, and gone backward the faster, the more he has spurr'd it forward. Esteem has wrought a like effect upon my Mind. My extraordinary inclination to shew that I honour you at an extraordinary rate, and to shew it in words that might not be altogether unworthy Mr.

Dryden's Perusal, incapacitates me to perform the very action to which it incites me, and Nature sinks in me under the fierce Effort.[1] But I hope you will have the Goodness to pardon a Weakness that proceeds from a Cause like this, and to consider that I had pleas'd you more if I had honour'd you less. Who knows but that yet I may please you, if you encourage me to mend my Fault? to which if you knew but the Place I am in, Charity would engage you, thô Justice could not oblige you. For I am here in a Desart, depriv'd of Company, and depriv'd of News; in a Place where I can hear nothing at all of the Publick, and what proves it ten times more a Desart, nothing at all of you: For all who are at present concern'd for their Countrey's Honour, hearken more after your Preparatives, than those for the next Campaigne.[2] These last may possibly turn to our Confusion, so uncertain are the Events of War; but we know that whatever you undertake must prove Glorious to England, and thô the French may meet with Success in the Field, by you we are sure to Conquer them. In War there are a thousand unlook'd for accidents which happen every day, and Fortune appears no where more like her self; but in a Combat of Wit, the more Humane Contention, and the more Glorious Quarrel, Merit will be always sure to prevail: And therefore, thô I can but hope that the Confederate Forces will give chase to De Lorges and Luxemburgh, I am very confident that Boileau and Racine will be forced to submit to you. Judge therefore if I, who very much love my Country, and who so much esteem you,

must not with a great deal of Impatience expect to hear
from you.

> I am,
> > Sir,
> > > Your most humble Servant
> > > [John Dennis]

Bushy-Heath,
Jan. 1693-4

Letter 30

DENNIS TO DRYDEN

Dear Sir,

You may see already by this Presumptuous
greeting, that Encouragement gives as much Assurance
to Friendship, as it imparts to Love. You may see too,
that a Friend may sometimes proceed to acknowledge
Affection, by the very same Degrees by which a Lover
declares his Passion. This last at first confesses Esteem,
yet owns no Passion but Admiration. But as soon as he
is Animated by one kind Expression, his Look, his Style,
and his very Soul are altered. But as Sovereign Beauties know very well, that he who confesses he Esteems
and Admires them, implies that he Loves them, or is
inclin'd to Love them; a Person of Mr. Dryden's
Exalted Genius, can discern very well, that when we
esteem him highly, 'tis Respect restrains us if we say
no more. For where great Esteem is without Affection,

'tis often attended with Envy, if not with Hate; which Passions Detract even when they Commend, and Silence is their highest Panegyric. 'Tis indeed impossible, that I should refuse to Love a Man, who has so often given me all the pleasure that the most Insatiable Mind can desire; when at any time I have been Dejected by Disappointments, or Tormented by cruel Passions, the recourse to your Verses has Calm'd my Soul, or rais'd it to Transports which made it contemn Tranquillity. But thô you have so often given me all the pleasure I was able to bear, I have reason to complain of you on this account, that you have confin'd my Delight to a narrower compass. Suckling, Cowley and Denham, who formerly Ravish'd me in ev'ry part of them, now appear tastless to me in most, and Waller himself with all his Gallantry, and all that Admirable Art of his turns, appears three quarters Prose to me. Thus 'tis plain that your Muse has done me an injury; but she has made me amends for it. For she is like those Extraordinary Women, who, besides the Regularity of their Charming Features, besides their engaging Wit, have Secret, Unaccountable, Enchanting Graces, which thô they have been long and often Enjoy'd, make them always new and always desirable. I return you my hearty thanks for your most obliging Letter.[1] I had been very unreasonable if I had Repin'd that the Favour arriv'd no sooner. 'Tis allowable to grumble at the delaying a payment, but to murmur at the deferring a Benefit, is to be impudently ungrateful beforehand. The Commendations which you give me, exceedingly sooth my

Vanity. For you with a breath can bestow or confirm
Reputation; a whole Numberless People Proclaims the
praise which you give, and the Judgments of three
mighty Kingdoms appear to depend upon yours. The
People gave me some little applause before,[2] but to
whom, when they are in the humour will they not give
it, and to whom when they are froward will they not
refuse it? Reputation with them depends upon Chance,
unless they are guided by those above them. They are
but the keepers, as it were, of the Lottery which Fortune sets up for Renown; upon which Fame is bound
to attend with her trumpet, and sound when Men draw
the Prizes. Thus I had rather have your Approbation
than the applause of Fame. Her commendation argues
good luck, but Mr. Dryden's implies desert. Whatever
low opinion I have hitherto had of my self, I have so
great a value for your Judgment, that, for the sake of
that, I shall be willing hence-forward to believe that I
am not wholly desertless; but that you may find me
still more Supportable, I shall endeavour to compensate
whatever I want in those glittering Qualities, by which
the World is dazled, with Truth, with Faith, and with
Zeal to serve you; qualities which for their rarity
might be objects of wonder, but that Men dare not appear to admire them, because their Admiration would
manifestly declare their want of them. Thus, Sir, let
me assure you, that thô you are acquainted with several
Gentlemen, whose Eloquence and Wit may capacitate
them to offer their service with more Address to you,
yet no one can declare himself, with greater Chearful-

ness, or with greater Fidelity, or with more profound Respect than my self.

Sir,

Your most, &c.

[John Dennis]

March 3, 1693

Letter 31

DRYDEN TO DENNIS

My Dear Mr. Dennis,

When I read a Letter so full of my Commendations as your last, I cannot but consider you as a Master of a vast Treasure, who having more than enough for your self, are forc'd to ebb out upon your Friends. You have indeed the best right to give them, since you have them in Propriety; but they are no more mine when I receive them, than the Light of the Moon can be allowed to be her own, who shines but by the Reflexion of her Brother. Your own Poetry is a more Powerful Example, to prove that the Modern Writers may enter into comparison with the Ancients, than any which Perrault[1] could produce in France; yet neither he, nor you who are a better Critick,[2] can persuade me that there is any room left for a Solid Commendation at this time of day, at least for me. If I undertake the Translation of Virgil, the little which I can perform will shew at least, that no Man is fit to write after him, in a barbarous

Modern tongue. Neither will his Machines be of any service to a Christian Poet. We see how ineffectually they have been try'd by Tasso, and by Ariosto. 'Tis using them too dully if we only make Devils of his Gods: As if, for Example, I would raise a Storm, and make use of Æolus, with this only difference of calling him Prince of the Air. What invention of mine would there be in this; or who would not see Virgil through me; only the same trick play'd over again by a Bungling Juggler? Boileau has well observed, that it is an easie matter in a Christian Poem, for God to bring the Devil to reason.[3] I think I have given a better hint for New Machines in my Preface to Juvenal; where I have particularly recommended two Subjects, one of King Arthur's Conquest of the Saxons, and the other of the Black Prince in his Conquest of Spain. But the Guardian Angels of Monarchys and Kingdoms, are not to be touch'd by every hand. A Man must be deeply conversant in the Platonick Philosophy, to deal with them: and therefore I may reasonably expect that no Poet of our Age will presume to handle those Machines for fear of discovering his own Ignorance; or if he should, he might perhaps be Ingrateful enough not to own me for his Benefactour.[4] After I have confess'd thus much of our Modern Heroick Poetry, I cannot but conclude with Mr. Rym[er], that our English Comedy is far beyond anything of the Ancients. And notwithstanding our irregularities, so is our Tragedy. Shakespear had a Genius for it; and we know, in spite of Mr. R— that Genius alone is a greater Virtue (if I may so call it) than all other Qualifications put together. You see what success this Learned Critick has found in the World, after his Blaspheming Shakespear. Almost all the Faults which he has discover'd are truly there; yet who will read Mr. Rym— or not read Shakespear? For my own part I reverence Mr. Rym—s Learning, but I detest his Ill Nature and his Arrogance. I indeed, and such as I, have reason to be afraid of him, but Shakespear has not. There is another part of Poetry in which the English stand almost upon an equal foot with the Ancients; and 'tis that which we call Pindarique; introduced but not perfected by our famous Mr. Cowley: and of this, Sir, you are certainly one of the greatest Masters. You have the Sublimity of Sense as well as Sound, and know how far the Boldness of a Poet may lawfully extend. I could wish you would cultivate this kind of Ode; and reduce it either to the same Measures which Pinder us'd, or give new Measures of your own. For, as it is, it looks like a vast Tract of Land newly discover'd. The Soil is wonderfully Fruitful, but un-manur'd, overstock'd with Inhabitants; but almost all Salvages, without Laws, Arts, Arms, or Policy. I re-member Poor Nat. Lee, who was then upon the Verge of Madness, yet made a Sober, and a Witty Answer to a Bad Poet, who told him, *It was an easie thing to write like a Madman: No*, said he, *'tis very difficult to write like a Madman, but 'tis a very easie matter to write like a fool*. Otway and He are safe by death from all At-tacks, but we poor Poets Militant (to use Mr. Cowley's Expression) are at the Mercy of Wretched Scribblers: And when they cannot fasten upon our Verses, they fall upon our Morals, our Principles of State and Religion.[5]

For my Principles of Religion, I will not justifie them to you. I know yours are far different. For the same Reason I shall say nothing of my Principles of State. I believe you in yours follow the Dictates of your Reason, as I in mine do those of my Conscience. If I thought my self in an Error, I would retract it; I am sure that I suffer for them; and Milton makes even the Devil say, That no Creature is in love with Pain. For my Morals, betwixt Man and Man, I am not to be my own Judge. I appeal to the World if I have Deceiv'd or Defrauded any Man: And for my private Conversation, they who see me every day can be the best Witnesses, whether or no it be Blameless and Inoffensive. Hitherto I have no reason to complain that Men of either Party shun my Company. I have never been an Impudent Beggar at the Doors of Noblemen: My Visits have indeed been too rare to be unacceptable; and but just enough to testifie my Gratitude for their Bounty, which I have frequently received, but always unask'd, as themselves will Witness. I have written more than I needed to you on this Subject: For I dare say you justifie me to your self. As for that which I first intended for the Principal Subject of this Letter, which is my Friend's Passion and his Design of Marriage,[6] on better consideration I have chang'd my Mind: For having had the Honour to see my Dear Friend Wycherly's Letter to him on that occasion, I find nothing to be added or amended. But as well as I love Mr. Wycherly, I confess I love my self so well, that I will not shew how much I am inferiour to him in Wit and Judgment; by undertaking any thing after him. There is

Moses and the Prophets in his Counsel. Jupiter and
Juno, as the Poets tell us, made Tiresias their Umpire,
in a certain Merry Dispute, which fell out in Heav'n
betwixt them. Tiresias you know had been of both
sexes, and therefore was a Proper Judge; our Friend
Mr. Wycherly is full as competent an Arbitrator: he
has been a Batchelor, and Marry'd man, and is now a
Widower. Virgil says of Ceneus,[7]

> Nunc Vir nunc Faemina Ceneus
> Rursus & in veterem fato revoluta figuram.

Yet I suppose he will not give any large commendations to his middle State:[8] Nor as the Sailer said, will
be fond after a Shipwrack to put to Sea again. If my
Friend will Adventure after this, I can but wish him
a good Wind, as being his and

My Dear Mr. Dennis,
Your most Affectionate
and most Faithful Servant,
John Dryden.

Letter 32

DRYDEN TO TONSON

Mr Tonson

Tis now three dayes since I have ended the
fourth Eneid; and I am this Morning beginning to
transcribe it; as you may do afterwards; for I am willing some few of my Friends may see it; & shall give

leave to you, to shew your transcription to some others, whose names I will tell you.[1] The paying Ned Sheldon the fifty pounds put me upon this speed;[2] but I intend not so much to overtoil my self, after the Sixth Book is ended, if the Second Subscriptions rise,[3] I will take so much the more time,[a] because the profit will incourage me the more; if not, I[b] must make the more hast;[c] yet allwayes with as much care as I am able. But However I will not fail in my paines of translating the Sixth Eneid with the same exactness as I have performd the Fourth: because that Book is my greatest Favourite. You know money is now very scrupulously receivd: in the last wch you did me the favour to change for my wife, besides the clipd money, there were at least forty shillings brass.[4] You may if you please come to me at the Coffee house this Afternoon, or at farthest tomorrow, that we may take care together, where & when I may receive the fifty pounds and the Guinneys;[5] which must be sometime this week.

I am Your Servant,
John Dryden.

Wednesday-morning

I have written to my Lord Lawderdail,[6] for his decorations.

---

[a] car *lined through after* the; *then immediately after* more, *both* care *and* paines *are lined through, and* time *is written between the lines*

[b] will *lined through after* I

[c] hast *written above* speed, *which is lined through*

Letter 33

DRYDEN TO TONSON

Saturday June the 8th

Mr Tonson

Tis now high time for me to think of my second Subscriptions: for the more time I have for collecting them, the larger they are like to be. I have now been idle just a fortnight, & therefore might have calld sooner on you, for the remainder of the first Subscriptions.[1] And besides, Mr Aston will be goeing into Cheshyre a week hence, who is my onely help, and to whom you are onely beholding for makeing the bargain betwixt us,[2] which is so much to my loss; but I repent nothing of it that is passd, but that I do not find my self capable of translating so great an Authour, & therefore feare to loose my own Credit, & to hazard your profit, which it wou'd grieve me if you shou'd loose, by your too good opinion of my Abilities. I expected to have heard of you this week, according to the intimation you gave me of it; but that failing, I must deferr it no longer than till the ensueing week because Mr Aston will afterwards be gone, if not sooner. Be pleasd to send me word what day will be most convenient to you; & be ready with the price of paper, & of the Books.[3] No matter for any Dinner; for that is a charge to you, & I care not for it. Mr Congreve may be with us, as a Common friend;[4] for as you know him for yours, I make not the least doubt, but he is much more mine.

Send an immediate answer, & you shall find me ready to
do all things wch become Your Servant

John Dryden

Letter 34

DRYDEN TO TONSON

Octob: the 29th

Mr Tonson

     Some kind of intercourse must be carryed on
betwixt us, while I am translateing Virgil. Therefore I
give you notice, that I have done the seaventh Eneid
in the Country: and intend some few days hence, to go
upon the Eigth: when that is finishd, I expect fifty
pounds, in good silver;[1] not such as I have had formerly. I am not obligd to take gold, neither will I;
not stay for it beyond four & twenty houres after it is
due. I thank you for the civility of your last letter in
the Country: but the thirty shillings upon every book
remains with me.[2] You always intended I shoud get
nothing by the Second Subscriptions, as I found from
first to last. And your promise to Mr Congreve, that
you had found a way for my benefit, which was an
Encouragement to my paines, came at last, for me[a] to
desire Sir Godfrey Kneller & Mr Closterman to gather
for me.[3] I then told Mr Congreve that I knew you too
well to believe you meant me any kindness: & he prom-

---

[a] for me *written between the lines*

isd me to believe accordingly of you, if you did not. But this is past, & you shall have your bargain if I live, and have my health: You may send me word what you have done in my business with the Earl of Derby.[4] And I must have a place for the Duke of Devonshyre.[5] Some of your friends will be glad to take back their three guinneys. The Countess of Macclesfield gave her money to Will Plowden[6] before Christmass; but he rememberd it not, & payd it not in. Mr Aston tells me my Lord Derby expects but one book. I find my Lord Chesterfield,[7] and my Lord Petre[8] are both left out; but my Lady Macclesfield must have a place, if I can possibly: and Will Plowden shall pay you in, three guinneys,[b] if I can obtain so much favour from you. I desire neither excuses nor reasons from you; for I am but too well satisfyd already. The Notes & Prefaces shall be short: because you shall get the more by saving paper.

John Dryden.

For Mr Jacob Tonson, Bookseller,
Att the Sign of the Judges Head, neare
Hercules Pillars In Fleet Street
These.

---

[b] three guinneys *written immediately after* the money, *which is lined through*

Letter 35

DRYDEN TO TONSON

Mr Tonson

Meeting Sir Ro: Howard at the play-house this morning, and asking him how he likd my Seaventh Eneid, He told me you had not brought it: He goes out of town tomorrow, being Saturday, after dinner. I desire you not to fail of carrying my manuscript for him to read in the Country. & desire him to bring it up with him, when he comes next to Town. I doubt you have not yet been with my Lord Chesterfield, and am in pain about it.

Y_{ors}

J Dryden.

Friday Night.

When you have leysure, I shou'd be glad to see how Mr Congreve & you have worded my propositions for Virgil:[1] When my Sonns play is acted I intend to translate again, if my health continue.[2] Some time next week let me heare from you, concerning the Propositions.

Letter 36

DRYDEN TO TONSON

Sir

I receivd your letter very kindly, because indeed I expected none; but thought you as very a tradesman as Bentley;[1] who has cursd our Virgil so heartily. I shall loose enough by your bill upon Mr Knight:[2] for after haveing taken it all in silver, & not in half Crowns neither, but shillings and sixpences, none of the money will go; for which reason I have sent it all back again, & as the less loss will receive it in guinneys at 29 shillings each.[3] Tis troublesome to be a looser; but it was my own fault to accept it this way, which I did to avoyd more trouble. I am not sorry that you will not allow any thing towards the Notes; for to make them good, wou'd have cost me half a yeares time at least. Those I write shall be onely Marginall to help the unlearned, who understand not the poeticall Fables. The Prefaces, as I intend them, will be somewhat more learned. It wou'd require seaven yeares to translate Virgil exactly. But I promise you once more, to do my best, in the four remaining Books, as I have hetherto done in the foregoing. Upon triall I find all of[a] your trade are Sharpers & you not more than others; therefore I have not wholly left you. Mr Aston does not blame you for getting as good a bargain as you cou'd, though I cou'd have gott an hunderd pounds more: and you might have spard almost all your trouble, if you

[a] of *written between the lines*

had thought fit to publish the proposalls for the first
Subscriptions:[4] for I have guinneas offerd me every
day, if there had been room; I believe modestly speaking, I have refusd already 25. I mislike nothing in
your letter therefore, but onely your upbraiding me
with the publique encouragement, & my own reputation
concernd in the Notes: when I assure you I cou'd not
make them to my mind, in less than half a yeares time.
Get the first half of Virgil transcribd as soon as possibly you can; that I may put the notes to it; & you
may have the other four books which lye ready for you,
when you bring the former; that the press may stay as
little as possibly it can.[5] My Lord Chesterfield has been
to visite me, but I durst say nothing of Virgil to him,
for feare there shou'd be no void place for him: if there
be, let me know;[6] & tell me whether you have made
room for the Duke of Devonshyre; haveing no silver
by me I desire my Lord Derbys money, deducting your
own. And let it be good, if you desire to oblige me who
am not your Enemy, & may be your friend

John Dryden.

Friday, forenoon.

　　Let me heare from you, as speedily as you can.

Letter 37

DRYDEN TO TONSON

Send word if you please, Sir, what is the most you will
give for my Sonns*a* play; that I may take the fairest
Chapman, as I am bound to do, for his benefit.[1] And
if you have any silver which will go, my wife will
be glad of it. I lost thirty shillings or more by the
last payment of fifty*b* pounds, wch you made at Mr
Knights.[2]

Yo^rs

J Dryden.

May 26th

Sir Ro: Howard writt me word, that if I cou'd make
any advantage by being payd in clippd money; He
woud change it in the Exchequer.

Letter 38

DRYDEN TO TONSON

Mr Tonson
    I had yesterday*a* morning two watches sent me
by Mr Tompion,[1] which I am to send my Sonns this
week. I cou'd not perswade him to take gold at any

a dr *lined through after* Sonns
b fifty *written above* thirty, *which is lined through*

a yesterday *written above* this, *which is lined through*

rate: But he will take*b* a Goldsmiths bill for two and twenty pounds, which is their price.² I desire you wou'd give him such a bill, and abate it out of the next fifty pounds which you are to pay me, when Virgil is finishd. Ten Eneids are finishd; & the ninth & tenth written out in my own hand. You may have them with the Eigth, which is in a foul copy, when you please to call for them; & to bring those which are transcribd. Mr Tompions man will be with me at four a clock in the Afternoon; & bring the watches, & must be payd at sight. I desire you therefore to procure a Goldsmiths bill, & let me have it before that houre, & send an answer by my Boy.

Yours. Jo: Dryden.

Thursday Morning

Letter 39

DRYDEN TO TONSON

Mr Tonson
    I have the remainder of my Northamptonshyre rents come up this weeke, and desire the favour of you, to receive them for me; from the Carrier of Tocester:¹ who lodges at the Castle in Smithfield. I suppose it is the same man, from whom you lately receivd them for my wife. Any time before ten a clock tomorrow morning, will serve the turne. If I were not deepely ingag'd

---

b take *written between the lines*

in my studyes, which will be finishd in a day or two, I
wou'd not put you to this trouble. I have inclosd my
Tenants letter to me, for you to shew the Carrier; & to
testify the summ, which is sixteen pounds, & about tenn
shillings; which the letter sets down.[2] Pray Sir, give
him an acquittance for so much receivd, as I suppose
you did last time.

I am

Your very Faithfull Servant,
John Dryden.

Wednesday Afternoon.
From the Coffee house
   Nov: 25th

Letter 40

DRYDEN TO TONSON

Sir

According to my promise I have sent you all
that is properly yours of my translation. I desire, as
you offerd, that it shou'd be transcribd in a legible
hand; & then sent back to me, for the last review; As
for some notes on the margins, they are not every
where; & when they are, are imperfect; so that you
ought not to transcribe them, till I make them com-
pleat. I feare you can scarcely make any thing of my
foul copy;[a] but it is the best I have. You see my hand

---

[a] my foul copy *written above* what I have written, *which is lined through*

failes me & therefore I write so short a letter. What I
wrote yesterday was too sharp; but I doubt it is all
true. Your Boys comeing upon so unseasonable a visit,
as if you were frighted for your self, discomposd me.

transcribe in very large paper; & leave a very large
margin.

Send your Boy for the foul copies & he shall have
them: for it will not satisfy me, to send them by my
own servant.   J Dryden.

I cannot yet find the first sheet of the first Eneid.
If it be lost, I will translate it over againe. But perhaps
it may be amongst the loose papers The fourth & ninth
Ecclogue which I have sent, are corrected in my wife's
printed Miscellany.[1]

Letter 41

DRYDEN TO THE EARL OF CHESTERFIELD

From Mr. John Dryden
The Poet, Lond. Febr 17th
$$\frac{96}{}\ [/97]$$

My Lord
I have hetherto wanted confidence to give your
Lordship the trouble of a letter which I design'd almost a year together:[1] And am now forc'd to take this
opportunity or wholly loose it. My Translation of
Virgil is already in the Press and I can not possibly
deferr the publication of it any Longer than Midsummer Term at farthes. I have hinder'd it thus long in

hopes of his return, for whom, and for my Conscience
I have sufferd, that I might have layd my Authour at
his feet:[2] But now finding that Gods time for ending
our miseries is not yet, I have been advis'd to make
three severall Dedications, of the Eclogues, the Georgics, and the Eneis. The Eclogues have been desired a
year ago by my Lord Clifford; whose father the Treasurer was my Patron,[3] the Eneids, by the Marquess of
Normanby,[4] and if I durst presume so farr, I would
humbly offer the Georgiques to your Lordships patronage. They are not I confess the most specious part
of Virgil, but in revenge they are his Masterpiece in
which he has not onely out done all other Poets, but
him self. Accordingly I have labour'd and I may say
I have cultivated the Georgiques with more care than
any other part of him, and as I think my self with more
success. Tis suitable to the retir'd life which you have
chosen, and to your studies of Philosophy: From the
first hour since I have had the happiness of being
know to your Lordship I have alwayes prefer'd you in
my poor esteem to any other Nobleman and that in all
respects. And you may please to believe me as an honest man, that I have not the least consideration of any
profit in this Address, but onely of honouring my self
by dedicating to you. By this time My Lord you may
perceive why I have been solicitous to procure the favour of your being one of the subscribers to this Worke:
And, to return to the beginning of my Letter, twas
upon a just diffidence of my success in this presumption
that I have humourd my natural bashfulness, in not
addressing to you sooner, But as becoming Women must

speak at last or loose their longing so I am constrain'd
to beg that I may not miscarry of my translation, who
am with all manner of humility

Your Lordships most obedient Servant
John Dryden.

Letter 42

THE EARL OF CHESTERFIELD TO DRYDEN

My answer to the former
Feb the $\dfrac{18}{97}$

Sr:

When I consider that the greatest men are desirous of being distinguished by some marke of your
esteem, I am surpris'd at the obligation that you have
layd upon me by intending (as you mention) to place
my name before some of your works.

It looks as if you were tired with the Court,[1] and
would now think of a Hermitage or of a country Gentleman, who being in no post whereby he may merit such
a favour, must value it the more, as proceeding from no
other motive than your kindness which I shall always
indeavour to deserve by being with great reality

Sr:

Your most humble Servant
Chesterfield

Letter 43

DRYDEN TO TONSON

Mr Tonson

I desire you woud let Mr Pate[1] know, I can print no more names of his Subscribers than I have money for, before I print their names. He has my acknowledgement[a] of ten guineas receivd from him; & as I told you I owe him for above three yards of fine cloath. Let him reckon for it; & then there will remain the rest for me, out of the ten more names, wch He has given in. If he has not money by him let him blott out as many of his names as He thinks good, & print onely those for wch he pays, or strikes off, in adjusting the Accounts betwixt me & him. This is so reasonable on both sides, that He cannot refuse it. but I would have all things ended now,[b] because I am to deal with a Draper, who is of my own perswasion; & to whom I have promisd my Custome.

Y^{ors}   John Dryden.

Tuesday Morning
   July the 6th
   1697

I have sent to My Tailour, & he sends me word, that I had three yards and half Elle of cloath from Mr Pate: I desire he woud make his price & deduct so much, as it comes to & make even for the rest, with ready money: as also that he woud send word, what the name

---

^a acknowledgement *written immediately after* receipt, *which is lined through*
^b now, *written between the lines*

was, for whom Sam: Atkins left him to make account for.[2]

For Mr. Tonson
These

Letter 44

THE EARL OF CHESTERFIELD TO DRYDEN

> To Mr. Dryden upon his Dedication of his translation of Virgils Georgics to me. Aug. the 10th and sending me the book. 97

Sr:

Tho I have never been ambitious of being obliged by many men, yet I am very much pleasd with the being so by Mr. Dryden. Not out of vanity in having my inconsiderable name placed (by so great a man) in the front of one of his Works, but because it gives the World a testimony of his freindship to me. I confess that I have alwayes esteem'd you the Homer of this Age, and I am sure that you have one advantage far above him, for he never shin'd much but in the darke, I mean till he was dead, and you have had that glory the greatest part of your life. But I do not pretend to offer the incence of prase, to him who is the best teacher of others how to give it; my intention being onely at this time to express some part of my resentments[1] for the unvaluable Present that you have made

me; and to desire your acceptance (by this bearer) of
a small mark of those respects[2] which shall ever be payd
you by

Sr

Your most humble servant
Chesterfield

Letter 45

DRYDEN TO THE EARL OF CHESTERFIELD

Mr. Dreydens answer to
my letter on the other
side Aug. the 18
                  1697

My Lord

   I can not pretend to acknowledg, as I ought, the
noble present which I have receiv'd from your Lordship, any more, than I can pretend to have deserv'd it.
I will not think, that, like Sylla,[1] you rewarded a bad
Poet and at the same time commanded him to write no
more: for the greatest vallue, I can put upon my selfe
is your favourable opinion of my Verses. I am glad that
they have pleas'd the World; but I am proud that they
have pleas'd your Lordship. By the Largeness of your
present, I must conclude that you considered who gave
and not who was to receive; and I know but one, who
made this reflection before your Lordship, and that was
Alexander. I am sure I need not say that I have

avoided flattery in my Dedication; for your character
was established with all, who had the honour of knowing you. I have onely spread it, amongst those, who
had not that happiness, as being from the bottom of
my heart, and without poetry

Your Lordships most obedient and most
obliged servant

John Dryden

Letter 46

DRYDEN TO SIR WILLIAM TRUMBULL

August 18

Sir

Being just ready to take Coach for the Country,
two of my best friends who have contributed very much
to my recovery,[1] have requested me to give you this
trouble in behalf of their Brother Mr Metcalf,[2] who is
commanded to appear tomorrow before the Councill
for printing a pamphlet of two sheets, in Latine, concerning a project of some of our Clergy to live in Common, that thereby they might be helpfull to Such of
our Communion who are in want. My Lord Archbishop
is pleased to represent this action as dangerous, for my
part I can say nothing of it, because I have not read it;
but I humbly request your moderation in it; & what
favour you can give, upon a just hearing of it. He is a

Young man & this his first offence, as, I hope, it will be
his last. I know you are instructed in the Cause, & I
petition for no more than what I may hope from the
known Candour of your Nature, that upon asking pardon & promising to offend no more, He may be for-
given, at the humble Suit of, Sir

Your most obedient obliged Servant

John Dryden

Letter 47

DRYDEN TO HIS SONS

[Sept. the] *a* 3d, our stile

[Dear Sons,

    Being now at Sir William Bowyer's in the] *a*
country[1] I cannot write at large, bec[ause I find my self
somewhat indisposed] *a* with a cold, & am thick of heareing rather worse than I was in town! I am glad to find
by your Letter of July 26th your stile, that you are
both in health: but wonder you shou'd think me so
negligent as to forget to give you an account of the
Ship, in wch your parcell is to come. I have written to
you two or three Severall Letters, concerning it; wch I
have sent by safe hands, as I told you, & doubt not but
you have them, before this can arrive to you. Being out
of Town, I have forgotten the Ship's name, wch your
mother will enquire and put it in her letter, wch is

---

  *a Manuscript is slightly torn and indistinct; words in brackets are supplied
from Malone.*

joynd with mine. But the Master's name I remember:
He is calld Mr Ralph Thorp; the Ship is bound to
Leghorn, consigned to Mr Peter & Mr. Tho: Ball
Merchants. I am of your opinion that by Tonsons
meanes, almost all our Letters have miscarryed for this
last yeare.[2] But however he has missd of his design in
the Dedication: though He had prepard the Book for it:
for in every figure of Eneas, he has causd him to be
drawn like K. William, with a hookd Nose. After my
return to Town, I intend to alter a play of Sir Robert
Howards, written long since, & lately put by him into
my hands: tis calld The Conquest of China by the
Tartars. It will cost me six weeks study, with the probable benefit of an hunderd pounds.[3] In the meane time
I am writeing a Song for St Cecilia's feast, who you
know is the Patroness of Musique.[4] This is troublesome, & no way beneficiall: but I coud not deny the
Stewards of the feast, who came in a body to me, to
desire that kindness; one of them being Mr Bridgman,[5]
whose parents are your Mothers friends. I hope to
send you thirty guineas, betwixt Michaelmass & Christmass of wch I will give you an account, when I come to
Town. I remember the Counsell you give me in your
letter: but dissembling, though lawfull in some Cases,
is not my talent: yet for your sake I will struggle, with
the plain openness of my nature, & keep in my just
resentments against that degenerate Order.[6] In the
mean time, I flatter not my self with any manner of
hopes. But do my duty & suffer for God's sake, being
assurd before hand, never to be rewarded, though the
times shoud alter. Towards the latter end of this

Moneth, September, Charles will begin to recover his
perfect health, according to his Nativity, wch casting it
my self, I am sure is true, & all things hetherto have
happend accordingly to the very time that I pred[icted
them: I hope at the same time to recover more] *a* health
according to my Age. R[emember me to poor Harry,
whose prayers I earnestly] *a* desire.[7] My Virgil suc-
ceeds in [the World beyond its desert or my Expectation. You] *a* know the profits might have been more,
but neither my conscience nor honour wou'd suffer me
to take them: but I never can repent of my Constancy;
since I am thoroughly perswaded of the justice of the
laws, for which I suffer. It has pleasd God to raise up
many friends to me amongst my Enemyes; though they
who ought to have been my friends, are negligent of
me. I am calld to dinner, & cannot go on with this
letter; wch I desire you to excuse, & am

Your most affectionate Father
John Dryden.

[To this letter Lady Elizabeth added the following:]

[My] *a* deare sonns I sent your Letter emedietly
to your father affter I had read it as you will find by
his: I have not [room] *a* to say much havinge writ a
former Letter to you datted the 27 of August your
father being then out of town he writs me word he is

---

*a Manuscript is slightly torn and indistinct; words in brackets are supplied
from Malone.*

much at woon as to his health: and his defnese is not
wores but much as he was when he was heare; he ex-
preses a great desire to see my deare Charlles: and
trully I see noe reason why you should not both come
together, to be a comfort to woon another. and to us
both: if the king of france includ Ingland in the peace
for you doe but just make shift to Live wheare you are:
and soe I hope you may doe heare: for I will Leaf noe
ston unturnd to help my beloved sonns: if I cane I will
send this Letter by the same way it came that is it was
brought me from woon Mr Galowway who corresponds
with Rozzie: I payd woon and Sixpence for it and did
offer to pay him what he demanded soe that he would
take care the might come saf to your handes: I Long
tell I heare my dear Charlles is better. I have onlly
room to tell you the names of the Merchantes your
parcell went in You are to demand them of Mr. Rob-
bert Ball & Thommas Ball in Livorno: You are not to
pay any charges for the box for the port of London if
the have demanded any of you send word to me what
it is: for otherwayes wee shall pay twice for them: and
this Mr Walkedon telles me with his service to you
both farweell my deare children God Allmighty keep
you in his protection for that is the wishes and prayers
of your most affec^t Mother that sends her Blesinge to
you all: not forgeting my sonn Harry, whose prayers I
desire for a comfortabell Meetinge I hope I may have
some better thinges: against you come then what is sent
you in that box theare being nothing considarabell but
my deare Jackes play: who I desire in his next to me to

give me a true account how my deare Sonn Charlles is
head dus for I can be at noe rest tell I heare he is better
or rather thorroly well which I dally pray for.

Al Illustrissimo Sig^re
Carlo Dryden, Camariere
d'Honore A S.S.
In Roma
Franca per Mantona

Letter 48

DRYDEN TO TONSON

Mr Tonson

I thank you heartily for the sherry; it was as
you sayd, the best of the kind I ever dranke. I have
found the Catalogue you desire, of the Subscribers
names, you left with me; & have sent them to you inclosd. Remember in the Copy of Verses for St. Cecilia,
to alter the name of Lais, wch is twice there, for Thais;
those two Ladyes were Contemporaryes, wch caused that
small mistake.[1] I wish you cou'd tell me how to send
My Sonns our Virgil, wch you gave me; & should be
glad if you coud put me in a way of remitting thirty
guineas to Rome; wch I woud pay heer, for my Sonns
to have the vallue there, according as the Exchange
goes; any time this fortnight, will be soon enough to

send the money: the Book I know will require a longer space, because ships go not for Italy every day.

I am

Your humble Servant

John Dryden.

I hear Tom Brown is comeing out upon me.[2]

Letter 49

DRYDEN TO TONSON

Mr. Tonson,

I have broken off my Studies from The Conquest of China,[1] to review Virgil, and bestowd nine entire days upon him. You may have the printed Copy you sent me to-morrow morning, if you will come for it yourself; for the Printer is a beast, and understands nothing I can say to him of correcting the press.— Dr. Chetwood[2] claims my promise of the Ode on St. Cecilia's Day; which I desire you to send him (according to the parliament phrase) forthwith. My wife says you have broken your promise, about the picture, and desires it speedily: the rest I will tell you when you come.

Yo[rs]

John Dryden.

Letter 50

DRYDEN TO TONSON

Mr Tonson

You were no sooner gone, but I felt in my pocket, & found my Lady Chudleighs verses;[1] which this Afternoon I gave Mr Walsh to read in the Coffee house. His opinion is the same with mine, that they are better than any wch are printed before the Book: so thinks also Mr Wycherley. I have them by me; but do not send them, till I heare from My Lord Clifford, whether My Lady will put her name to them or not. therefore I desire they may be printed last of all the Copyes, & of all the Book.^a[2] I have also written this day to Mr Chetwood, & let him know, that the Book is immediately goeing to the press again. My opinion is, that the printer shou'd begin with the first Pastoral; & print on to the end of the Georgiques, or farther, if occasion be, till Dr Chetwood corrects his preface,[3] wch He writes me word is printed very false. You cannot take too great care of the printing this Edition, exactly after my Amendments: for a fault of that nature will disoblige me Eternally. I am glad to heare from all Hands, that my Ode is esteemd the best of all my poetry, by all the Town: I thought so my self when I writ it but being old, I mistrusted my own Judgment. I hope it has done you service, & will do more. You told me not, but the Town says, you are printing Ovid de Arte Amandi;[4] I know my Translation is very un-

---

^a & of all the Book *written between the lines*

correct: but at the same time I know no body else can do it better, with all their pains. If there be any loose papers in the Virgil I gave you this Morning, look for them, & send them back by my Man. I miss not any yet: but 'tis possible some may be left; because I gave you the Book, in a hurry. I vow to God, if Evering-ham[5] takes not care of this Impression, He shall never print any thing of mine heerafter: for I will write on, since I find I can. I desire you to make sure of the three pounds of snuff, the same of which I had one pound from you. When you send it any Morning, I will pay for it altogether. But this is not the business of this letter.— When you were heer, I intended to have sent an Answer to poor Charles his letter; but I had not then the letter wch my Chirurgeon[6] promisd me, of his advice, to prevent a Rupture wch He fears. Now I have the Surgeons Answer, wch I have inclosed in my letter to my Sonn: this is a business of the greatest consequence in the world: for you know how I love Charles:[7] And therefore I write to you with all the Earnestnesse of a father, that you will procure Mr Francia to inclose it, in his pacquet this week:[8] for a week lost may be my Sonns ruine: whom I intend to send for, next Summer, without his Brother, as I have writ-ten him word: and if it please God that I must dye of over study, I cannot spend my life better, than in saving his. I vallue not any price for a double Letter: let me know it, & it shall be payd: for I dare not trust it by the Post: being satisfyd by Experience, that Ferrard[9] will do by this, as He did by two letters which I sent My Sonns, about my Dedicating to the King, of which they receivd neither.[10] If you cannot go your self, then send a Note to Signior Francia, as earnestly as you can write it, to beg that it may go this Day, wch I meane Friday. I need not tell you, how much heerein you will oblige

Your Friend and Servant
J. D.

Letter 51

DRYDEN TO JOHN CARYLL

Sr:

'Tis the part of an honest man to be as good as his Word, butt you have been better: I expected but halfe what I had, and that halfe, not halfe so Good. Your Veneson had three of the best Qualities, for it was both fatt, large & sweet. To add to this you have been pleased to invite me to Ladyholt, and if I could promise my Self a year's Life, I might hope to be happy in so sweet a place, & in the Enjoyment of your good company.[1] How God will dispose of me, I know not: but I am apt to flatter my Self with the thoughts of itt, because I very much desire itt, and am Sr with all manner of Acknowlegment

Y^r. most obliged and most faithful Servant
John Dryden.

July 21, 1698

Letter 52

DRYDEN TO MRS. STEWARD

Saturday, Octob. 1st-98.

Madam

You have done me the honour to invite so often that it wou'd look like want of respect to refuse it any longer. How can you be so good, to an old decrepid Man who can entertain you with no discourse which is worthy of your good sense & who can onely be a trouble to you in all the time he stays at Cotterstock? Yet I will obey your Commands as far as possible I can; and give you the inconvenience you are pleas'd to desire: At least for the few days which I can spare from other necessary business; which requires me at Tichmarsh Therefore if you please to send your Coach on Tuesday next by Eleven a clock in the Morning I hope to wait on you before dinner. Ther' is onely one more trouble, wch I am almost ashamd to name. I am obliged to visit My Cousin Dryden of Chesterton some time next week, who is nine miles from hence,[1] and onely five from you. If it be with your convenience to spar' me your Coach thether for a day, the rest of my time till Monday is at your service & I am sorry for my own sake it cannot be any longer this year because I have some visits after my return hether, which I cannot avoyd. But if it please God to give me life & health, I may give you occasion another time to repent of your kindness by making you weary of my Company. My sonne kesses your hand.[2]

Be pleased to give his humble service to my Cousin
Steward, and mine who am
                    Madam
          Your most obedient, obleged Servant
                  John Dryden

Letter 53

DRYDEN TO ELMES STEWARD

My Honourd Cousin
          I shou'd have receivd your Letter with too much
satisfaction, if it had not been allayd with the bad news
of my Cousin your wife's indisposition; which yet I
hope will not continue. I am sure if care & love will
contribute to her health, she will want neither from so
tender a Husband as you are: & indeed you are both
worthy of each other. You have been pleasd, each of
you, to be kind to my Sonn & me your poor Relations,
without any merit on our side, unless you let our gratitude pass for our desert, And now you are pleasd to
invite another trouble on your self: which our bad Company may possibly draw upon you next year, if I have
life & health, to come into Northamptonshyre. And that
you will please not to make so much a stranger of me
another time. I intend my wife shall tast the plover
you did me the favour to send me. If either your Lady,
or you shall at any time honour me with a letter, My

house is in Gerard Street, the fifth door on the left hand, comeing from Newport Street.[1] I pray God I may heare better news of both your healths, & of my good cousin Creeds,[2] and my Cousin*a* Dorothy,[3] than I have had, while I was in this Country. I shall languish till you send me word; & I assure you I write this without poetry, who am from the bottome of my Heart

My Honourd Cousins most obliged
Humble Servant
John Dryden.

My sonn & I kiss my Cousin Stewards hand, & give our service, to your sister, and pretty Miss Betty.[4]

    For My Honourd Cousin
    Elmes Steward Esq
    att Cotterstock.

Letter 54

DRYDEN TO MRS. STEWARD

Nov: 23d, 1698

Madam
    To take acknowledgments of favours, for favours done you, is onely yours. I am always on the receiveing hand: & you who have been pleasd to be troubled so long with my bad Company, in stead of forgiveing, which is all I cou'd expect, will turn it to a kindness on my side. If your House be often so molested, you will

a my Cousin *written above* Mrs, *which is lined through*

have reason to be weary of it, before the ending of the
Year: & wish Cotterstock were planted in a desart, an
hundred miles off from any Poet. After I had lost the
happiness of your Company, I cou'd expect no other
than the loss of my health, which follow'd, according to
the proverb, that Misfortunes seldome come alone. I
had no woman to visite,[1] but the Parson's wife; & she
who was intended by Nature, as a help meet for a deaf
Husband, was somewhat of the loudest, for my Conversation; & for other things, I will say no more, than that
she is just your Contrary: and an Epitome of her own
Country. My Journey to London, was yet more unpleasant than my abode at Tichmarsh: for the Coach
was Crowded up with an old woman, fatter than any of
my Hostesses on the Rode. I must confess she was for
the most part Silent, unless it were, that sometimes her
backside talkd; & that discourse was not over savoury to
the Nose. Her weight made the Horses travell very
heavily; but to give them a breathing time, she wou'd
often stop us; & plead some necessity of Nature, & tell
us we were all flesh and blood: but she did this so frequently, that at last we conspird against her; & that she
might not be inconvenienc'd by staying in the Coach,
turnd her out in a very dirty place, where she was to
wade up to the Anckles, before she cou'd reach the next
hedge. When I was ridd of her, I came sick home: &
kept my House, for three weeks together; but by advice
of my Doctour, takeing twice the bitter draught, with
Sena in it, & looseing at least twelve Ounces of blood, by
Cupping on my Neck, I am just well enough, to go
abroad in the Afternoon: but am much afflicted, that I

have you a Companion of my Sickness: though I scapd
with one cold fit of an Ague; & yours I feare is an Intermitting feavour. Since I heard nothing of your
father, whom I left ill, I hope he is recoverd of his reall
sickness; & that your sister is well of hers, which was
onely in Imagination. My wife, & sonn return you
their most humble*a* service; & I give mine to my cousin
Steward. Madam, Your most obliged, & most obedient
Servant

John Dryden.

For Mrs. Steward, Att Cotterstock
Neare Oundle, In the County of
Northampton, These:
To be left with the postmaster of
Oundle; & thence conveyd.

Letter 55

DRYDEN TO MRS. STEWARD

Dec. 12th-98.

Madam

All my Letters being nothing but Acknowledgments of your favours to me, 'tis no wonder if they are
all alike: for they can but Express the same thing; I
being eternally the Receiver; and you the Giver. I wish
it were in my power to turn the skale on the other hand,
that I might see, how you, who have so Excellent a wit,
cou'd thank on your Side. Not to name my self, & my

---

a humble *written between the lines*

wife, My Sonn Charles is the great Commender of your last receivd Present: who being of late somewhat indisposd, uses[a] to send for some of the same sort, which we call heer Marrow Puddings, for his Suppers: but the tast of yours, has so spoyld his Markets heer, that there is not the least Comparison betwixt them. You are not of an Age to be a Sybill; & yet I think you are a Prophetess: for the direction on your Basket was for him; and He is likely to enjoy the greatest part of them: for I always think the young are more worthy than the old: Especially since you are One of the former Sort; & that He mends upon your Medicine. I am very glad to hear my Cousin your Father[1] is comeing, or come to Town: perhaps this Ayr, may be as Beneficiall to him as it has been to me; but you tell me nothing of your own Health; & I fear Cotterstock[2] is too Agueish for this Season. My wife & Sonn, give you their most humble thanks and Service; as I do mine, to my cousin Steward; and am Madam,

> Your most Oblig'd, Obedient
> Servant,
> John Dryden.

> For Mrs Steward
> Att Cotterstock, near
> Oundle, in the County of
> Northton,
> These
> To be left with the Postmaster
> of Oundle.

[a] uses *written above* usd of late, *which is lined through*

Letter 56

DRYDEN TO THE DUKE OF ORMOND

The first day of Winter, 1698.

May it please y^r Grace

What Ireland was before y^r coming Thither I cannot tell, but I am sure you have brought over one manufacture thither wch is not of ye growth of ye country, and that is beauty. But at the same time, you have impoverished y^r Native Land by taking more away y^n you have left behind. We Jacobites have no more reason to thank you than we have our present King who has enriched Holland wth the wealth of England. If this be all the effect of his going over the water for a whole Summer together and of y^r Graces leaving us for a much longer time, we have reason to complain if not of both, yet at least of one of you for the Sun has never Shone on us since you went into Eclipse on Ireland, and if we have another Such a yeare we shall have a famine of Beauty as well as Bread, for if the last be the Staff of Life to the rest of the World the first is so to the Nation of Poets; who feed only at the eyes. But you Plantagenets, never think of these mean Concernm^{ts}; the whole race of you have been given to make voyages into ye Holy Land to Conquer Infidells or at least to Subdue France without caring w^t becomes of y^r naturall subjects ye poor English. I think we must remonstrate to you y^t we can no longer live without you: For so our Ancestours have done to some of y^r Family w^n they have been too long abroad And besides who knows but God who can do all things wch seem impossible to us may raise up another beauty in y^r Absence who may dispute y^r Kingdome with you for thus also has y^r Predecessour Richard Coeur de Leon been servd when his B^r John whose christned name I bear while he was takeing Jerusalem from ye Turks was likely to have Usurpd Eng^d from him And I cannot promise for ye fidelity of a Country which is not over famous for that vertue. The product o[f] Ireland will onely serve to warm my Body as it does this Winter by y^r Graces favour to me but I cannot beare to be cold at heart and the older I am the more need I have of the Sun to comfort me for wch reason I humbly advise you to re-turne next Spring wth the first Swallow though you fal-sifie the Proverb for then one Swallow will make a Spring at least to him who is

> Y^r Graces most Obliged and most Obedient Servant
> John Dryden.

Letter 57

DRYDEN TO MRS. STEWARD

Candlemass-Day, 1698[/99]

Madam,

Old Men are not so insensible of beauty, as it may be, you young ladies think. For my own part, I must needs acknowledge that your fair eyes had made me your slave before I receivd your fine presents. Your letter puts me out of doubt that they have lost nothing of their lustre, because it was written with your own hand; and not heareing of a feavour or an ague, I will please my self with the thoughts that they have wholly left you. I wou'd also flatter my self with the hopes of waiting on you in Cotterstock some time next summer; but my want of health may perhaps hinder me. But if I am well enough to travell as farr north as Northamptonshyre, you are sure of a guest, who has been too well us'd, not to trouble you again.

My sonn, of whom you have done me the favour to enquire, mends of his indisposition very slowly; the ayr of England not agreeing with him hetherto so well as that of Italy. The Bath is propos'd by the Doctours, both to him and me: but we have not yet resolv'd absolutely on that journey; for that city is so closs and so ill situated, that perhaps the ayr may do us more harm than the waters can do us good: for which reason we intend to try them heer first;[1] and if we find not the good effect which is promis'd of them, we will save our selves the pains of goeing thether. In the mean time, betwixt my intervalls of physique and other remedies which I am useing for my gravell, I am still drudging on: always a Poet, and never a good one. I pass my time sometimes with Ovid, and sometimes with our old English poet, Chaucer; translating such stories as best please my fancy; and intend besides them to add somewhat of my own: so that it is not impossible, but ere the summer be pass'd, I may come down to you with a volume in my hand,[2] like a dog out of the water, with a duck in his mouth. As for the rarities you promise, if

beggars might be choosers, a part of a chine of honest
bacon wou'd please my appetite more than all the marrow puddings; for I like them better plain; having a
very vulgar stomach.— My wife and your Cousin,
Charles, give you their most humble service, and thanks
for your remembrance of them. I present my own to
my worthy Cousin, your husband, and am, with all
respect,

Madam,

Your most obliged Servant,

John Dryden.

For Mrs. Stewart,
att Cotterstock,
in Northamptonshyre,
These.
To be left with the Postmaster of Oundle.

Letter 58

DRYDEN TO MRS. STEWARD

Thursday Feb: 9th

−98 [/99]

Madam

For this time I must follow a bad Example, &
send you a shorter Letter than your short one: you
were hinderd by the dancers; & I am forc'd to dance
attendance all this Afternoon, after a troublesome business, so soon as I have written this & seald it. Onely I

can assure you that your father & mother, & all your Relations are in health; or were yesterday, when I sent to enquire of their welfare. On Tuesday Night, we had a violent wind, wch blew down three of my chimneys, & dismantled all one side of my House, by throwing down the tiles. My Neighbours, & indeed all the Town, sufferd more or less; & some were killd. The Great Trees in St. James's Park, are many of them torn up from the roots; as they were before Oliver Cromwells death; & the late Queens: but your father had no damage. I sent my Man for the present you designd me: but he returnd empty handed: for there was no such man as Carter a Carrier, Inning at the Bear, & ragged Staff in^a Smithfield. Nor any one there, ever heard of such a person: by which I ghess that some body has deceivd you with a Counterfeited Name. Yet my obligations are the same; & the favour shall be always ownd, by Madam

Your most humble Servant & Kinsman
John Dryden.

For Mrs Stewart
att Cotterstock neare
Oundle, In the County
of Northampton
These
To be left with the Postmaster
of Oundle

---

^a in *written above* at, *which is lined through*

Letter 59

DRYDEN TO MRS. STEWARD

Madam

I have reason to be pleasd with writeing to you; because you are daily giveing me Occasions to be pleasd. The Present which you made me this week I have receivd: & it will be part of the treat I am to make to three of my friends, about Tuesday next: my Cousin Driden of Chesterton,[1] haveing been also pleasd to add to it, a turkey hen with Eggs, & a good young Goose; besides a very kind letter, & the News of his own good health, which I vallue more than all the rest; He being so noble a Benefactour to a poor, & so undeserveing a Kinsman, & one of another persuasion, in matters of Religion. Your Enquiry of his welfare, & sending also mine, have at once obligd both him and me. I hope my good Cousin Stewart will often visite him, especially before hunting goes out, to be a comfort to him in his sorrow, for the loss of his deare Brother,[2] who was a Most Extraordinary well Natur'd Man, & much my friend. Exercise I know is my Cousin Driden's life; & the oftner he goes out, will be the better for his health. We poor Catholiques daily expect a most Severe Proclamation to come out against us;[3] & at the same time are satisfyed, that the King is very Unwilling to persecute us; considering us to be but an handfull, & those disarmd: But the Archbishop of Canterbury is our heavy Enemy; & heavy He is indeed, in all respects.[4] This Day was playd a reviv'd Comedy of

Mr Congreve's calld the Double Dealer, which was never very takeing; in the play bill was printed,— Written by Mr Congreve; with Severall Expressions omitted: What kind of Expressions those were you may easily ghess; if you have seen the Monday's Gazette, wherein is the Kings Order, for the reformation of the Stage:[5] but the printing an Authours name, in a Play bill, is a new manner of proceeding, at least in England. When any papers of verses, in Manuscript,[a] which are worth your reading come abroad, you shall be sure of them; because being a Poetess yourself, you like those Entertainments. I am still drudgeing at a Book of Miscellanyes,[6] which I hope will be well enough. if otherwise, three-score & seaven may be pardon'd. Charles is not yet so well recoverd as I wish him: but I may say, without vanity, that his vertue & Sobriety, have made him much[b] belov'd, in all Companies both He & his Mother give you their most humble acknowledgments of your remembring them. Be pleasd to give mine to my Cousin Stewart, who am both his & your most oblig'd obedient Servant

John Dryden

March the 4th
    1698 [/99]

You may see I was in hast, by writeing on the wrong side of the Paper.

---

[a] *an illegible word lined through after* Manuscript
[b] *an illegible word lined through after* much

Letter 60

DRYDEN TO MRS. STEWARD

Tuesday, July the 11th

Madam

As I cannot accuse my Self, to have receivd any Letters from you without answer, so on the other side, I am obligd to believe it, because you say it. Tis true I have had so many fitts of Sickness & so much other unpleasant business, that I may possibly have receivd those favours, & deferrd my Acknowledgment, till I forgot to thank you for them. However it be, I cannot but Confess, that never was any Unanswering Man so Civilly reproachd by a fair Lady. I presum'd to send you word by your Sisters, of the trouble I intended you this Summer; & added a petition, that you wou'd please to order some small Beer to be brewd for me, without hops, or with a very inconsiderable quantity, because I lost my health last year, by drinking bitter beer at Tichmarsh. It may perhaps be Sour, but I like it not the worse, if it be small Enough. What els I have to request, is onely the favour of your Coach, to meet me at Oundle, & to convey me to you: of which I shall not fail to give you timely Notice. My Humble Service attends my Cousin Stewart, & your relations at Oundle. My wife & Sonn, desire the same favour. And I am particularly, Madam, Your most Obedient Servant

John Dryden.

For Mrs Stewart, att
Cotterstock, neare Oundle,
Northamptonshyre
These
To be left with the Postmaster
of Oundle.

Letter 61

DRYDEN TO PEPYS

July the 14th, 1699.

Padron Mio,

I remember last year, when I had the honour of dining with you, you were pleas'd to recommend to me, the Character of Chaucer's Good Parson. Any desire of yours is a Command to me; and accordingly I have put it into my English, with such additions and alterations as I thought fit. Having translated as many Fables from Ovid, and as many Novills from Boccace and Tales from Chaucer,[1] as will make an indifferent large volume in folio, I intend them for the press in Michaelmass Term next.[2] In the mean time my Parson desires the favour of being known to you, and promises, if you find any fault in his character, he will reform it.[3] Whenever you please, he shall wait on you, and for the safer Conveyance, I will carry him in my pocket; who am

My *padrons* most obedient Servant,
John Dryden.

For Samuel Pepys, Esq.
Att his house in York-street,
These.

Letter 62

PEPYS TO DRYDEN

Friday, July 14, 1699.

Sir,

You truly have oblig'd mee; and possibly in saying so, I am more in earnest then you can readily think; as verily hopeing from this your copy of one good Parson, to fancy some amends made mee for the hourly offence I beare with from the sight of soe many lewd originalls.[1]

I shall with great pleasure attend you on this occasion, when ere you'l permit it; unless you would have the kindness to double it to mee, by suffering my coach to wayte on you (and who you can gayne mee ye same favour from) hither, to a cold chicken and a sallade, any *noone* after Sunday, as being just stepping into the ayre for 2 days. I am most respectfully

Your honord & obednt Servant,

S. P.

Letter 63
DRYDEN TO MRS. STEWARD

Madam

This is onely a word, to threaten you with a troublesome guest next week: I have taken places for my self & my Sonn in the Oundle Coach; which sets out on Thursday next, the tenth of this present August: & hope to wait on a fair Lady at Cotterstock, on Friday the Eleventh. If you please to let your Coach come to Oundle, I shall save my Cousine Creed the trouble of hers. All heer are your most humble Servants, & particularly an old Cripple, who calls him self, Your most obliged Kinsman & Admirer,

John Dryden

Saturday Aug: 5th
1699
For Mrs Stewart Att
Cotterstock, near Oundle
In Northamptonsh:
These
To be left, with the Postmaster
of Oundle.

Letter 64

DRYDEN TO MRS. STEWARD

Madam

Your goodness to me will make you sollicitous of my welfare since I left Cotterstock. My Journey has in general, been as happy, as it cou'd be, without the satisfaction & honour of your Company. Tis true the Master of the Stage Coach, has not been over civill to me: for he turnd us out of the Road, at the first step, & made us go to Pilton; there we took in a fair young Lady of Eighteen & her Brother a young Gentleman; they were related to the Trishams, but not of that Name: thence we drove to Higham, where we had an old serving woman, & a young fine Mayd: we din'd at Bletso, & lay at Silso, six miles beyond Bedford. there we put out the old woman, & took in Councellour Jennings[1] his Daughter; Her father goeing along in the Kittering Coach, or rideing by it, with other Company: We all din'd at Hatfield together; & came to Town safe, at 7 in the Evening. We had a young Doctour, who rode by our Coach, & seemd to have a smickering to our young Lady of Pilton & ever rode before to get dinner in a readiness: My Sonn Charles knew him formerly a Jacobite; & now goeing over to Antigoo,[2] with Colonel Codrington,[3] haveing been formerly in the West Indies. Which of our two young Ladies was the handsomer I know not. My Sonn likd the Councellours daughter best: I thought they were both equall. But, not goeing by Tichmarsh Grove, & afterwards by

Catworth, I missd my two Couple of Rabbetts, which my Cousin your father had given me to carry with me; & cou'd not see my Sister by the way:[4] I was likewise dissappointed of Mr Cole's Ribadavia wine:[5] but I am almost resolvd to sue the Stage Coach; for putting me six or seaven miles out of the way; wch He cannot justify. Be pleasd to accept my acknowledgment of all your favours, & my Cousin Stuarts; & by employing my Sonn & me in any thing you desire to have done, give us occasion to take our Revenge on our kind relations both at Oundle & Cotterstock. Be pleas'd, your father, your Mother, your two fair Sisters & your Brother may find my Sonns Service, & mine, made acceptable to them by your delivery, and believe me, to be, with all manner of gratitude, (give me leave to add all manner of[a] Adoration,)

Madam
Your most Obliged, Obedient Servant
John Dryden.

Sept: 28th

99.

For Mrs Stuart, Att
Cotterstock, near Oundle
In Northtonshyre,
These.
To be left with the Postmaster
of Oundle.

---

[a] *an illegible word lined through after* of

Letter 65

DRYDEN TO THE RIGHT HONOURABLE
CHARLES MONTAGUE

Sir

These verses[1] had waited on you with the former;[2] but they then wanted that Correction, which I
have since given them, that they may*a* the better endure
the Sight of so great a Judge & Poet. I am now in feare
that I have purgd them out of their Spirit; as our Master Busby, usd to whip a Boy so long, till he made him
a Confirmd Blockhead. My Cousin Driden saw them
in the Country; & the greatest Exception He made to
them, was a Satire against the Dutch valour, in the late
Warr. He desir'd me to omit it, (to use his Own
words) out of the respect He had to his Soveraign. I
obeyd his Commands; & left onely the praises, which
I think are due to the gallantry of my own Country-
men. In the description which I have made of a
Parliament Man, I think I have not onely drawn the
features of my worthy Kinsman, but have also given my
Own opinion, of what an Englishman in Parliament
oughto be; & deliver it as a Memorial of my own Principles to all Posterity. I have consulted the Judgment
of my Unbyassd friends, who have some of them the
honour to be known to you; & they think there is nothing which can justly give offence, in that part of the
Poem. I say not this, to cast a blind on your Judgment
(which I cou'd not do, if I indeavourd it) but to assure

a may *written between the lines*

you, that nothing relateing to the publique shall stand, without your permission. For it were to want Common sence, to desire your patronage, & resolve to disoblige you: and as I will not hazard my hopes of your protection by refusing to obey you in any thing, which I can perform with my conscience, or my honour; So I am very confident you will never impose any other terms on me. My thoughts at present are fixd on Homer: And by my translation of the first Iliad; I find him a Poet more according to my Genius than Virgil: and consequently hope I may do him more justice, in his fiery way of writeing; which, as it is liable to more faults, so it is capable of more beauties, than the exactness, & sobriety of Virgil. Since 'tis for my Country's honour as well as for my own,[3] that I am willing to undertake this task; I despair not of being encouragd in it, by your favour who am Sir

Your most Obedient Servant,
John Dryden.

Letter 66

DRYDEN TO MRS. STEWARD

Madam
    I pretend not to write to you: if I did, I should not have borrowd a corner in my Sonns letter: But even then, I shou'd have filld my paper, before I had emptyd my thoughts, for I can never express with words how

much your undeservd favours have wonn on me: Dr
Radclyff[1] calls Northamptonshyre a Shineing Country:
I doubt not but he means for Hospitality; & yet He has
never been at Cotterstock: The two young Gentlemen,
who sayd they were almost stervd with you, had better
fortune than I found, who can complain of nothing but
too much, & a variety of daintyes. But you it seems,
were spareing to them of your company, which had
certainly been thrown away upon them: that I confess,
I had, & of that onely I can never surfeit, who am with
all manner of respect and gratitude

Madam

Your most obligd kinsman

And most obedient Servant

John Dryden.

Be pleasd to give my most humble*a* service to my
Cousin Steward, his Sister, & all your little fair family.

Letter 67

DRYDEN TO MRS. STEWARD

Madam

Even your Expostulations are pleasing to me:
for though they shew you angry; yet they are not without many expressions of your kindness: & therefore I
am proud to be so chidden. Yet I cannot so farr aban-
don my own defence, as to confess any idleness or for-

a humble *written above the line*

getfulness on my part. What has hindred me from writing to you, was neither ill health, nor a worse thing ingratitude, but a flood of little businesses, which yet are necessary to my Subsistance, & of which I hopd to have given you a good account before this time; but the Court rather speaks kindly of me, than does any thing for me, though they promise largely:[1] & perhaps they think I will advance, as they go backward: in which they will be much deceivd: for I can never go an Inch beyond my Conscience & my Honour. If they will consider me as a Man, who have done my best to improve the Language, & Especially the Poetry, & will be content with my acquiescence under the present Government, & forbearing satire on it, that I can promise, because I can perform it: but I can neither take the Oaths, nor forsake my Religion, because I know not what Church to go to, if I leave the Catholique; they are all so divided amongst them selves in matters of faith, necessary to Salvation: & yet all assumeing the name of Protestants. May God be pleasd to open your Eyes, as he has opend mine:[2] Truth is but one; & they who have once heard of it, can plead no Excuse, if they do not embrace it. But these are things too serious, for a trifling Letter.— If you desire to heare any thing more of my Affars, the Earl of Dorsett, & your Cousin Montague have both seen the two Poems, to the Duchess of Ormond, & my worthy Cousin Driden: And are of opinion that I never writt better. My other friends, are divided in their Judgments which to preferr: but the greater part are for those to my dear Kinsman; which I have Corrected with so much care, that they will now be worthy of his Sight: & do neither of us any dishonour after our death. There is this day to be acted a New tragedy, made by Mr Hopkins;[3] & as I believe in rhime. He has formerly written a play in verse calld Boadicea, which you fair Ladyes likd: & is a poet who writes good verses without knowing how, or why; I mean he writes naturally well, without art or learning, or good sence. Congreve is ill of the Gout at Barnet Wells: I have had the honour of a visite from the Earl of Dorsett, & din'd with him.[4] Matters in Scotland are in a high ferment; & next door to a breach betwixt the two Nations: But they say from Court, that France & we are hand & glove. tis thought the King will endeavour to keep up a standing Army; & make the stirr in Scotland his pretence for it: My Cousin Driden, & the Country Party, I suppose will be against it: for when a Spirit is raisd, 'tis hard conjureing him down again. You may see I am dull by my writeing news: but it may be My Cousin Creed may be glad to hear what I believe is true, though not very pleasing: I hope He recovers health in the Country, by his stay-ing so long in it. My Service to my Cousin Stuart; & all at Oundle. I am, faire Cousine

Your most Obedient Servant
John Dryden.

Nov: 7th

For Mrs Stuart, Att
Cotterstock, near Oundle
In Northamptonshyre
These.
To be left At the posthouse
In Oundle:

Letter 68
DRYDEN TO ELIZABETH THOMAS

Madam,

The Letter you were pleased to direct for me, to be left at the Coffee-house last Summer, was a great Honour; and your Verses were, I thought, too good to be a*a* Woman's; some of my Friends to whom I read them were of the same Opinion. 'Tis not over gallant, I must confess, to say this of the fair Sex; but most certain it is, that they generally write with more Softness than Strength. On the contrary, you want neither Vigour in your Thoughts, nor force in your Expressions, nor Harmony in your Numbers, and methinks I find much of Orinda*b* in your Manner (to whom I had the Honour to be related, and also to be Known.)[1] But I continued not a Day in the Ignorance of the Person to whom I was obliged; for, if you remember, you brought the Verses to a Bookseller's Shop, and enquired there, how they might be sent to me. There happened to be in the same Shop a Gentleman, who hearing you speak of me, and seeing a Paper in your Hand, imagined it was a Libel against me, and had you watched by his Servant, till he knew both your Name, and where you lived, of which he sent me word immediately. Tho' I have lost his Letter, yet I remember you live some where about St.*c* Giles's, and are an only Daughter.

a A Pastoral, hereafter mentioned [Footnote in the 1727 text.]
b The celebrated Mrs. Katherine Philips [Footnote in the 1727 text.]
c Corinna then lived in Dyott-Street, in St. Giles's in the Fields, as did also Mr. Dryden in the same Parish [Footnote in the 1727 text.][2]

You must have passed your Time in Reading much
better Books than mine; or otherwise you could not
have arrived at so much Knowledge as I find you have.
But whether Sylph or Nymph I Know not; Those fine
Creatures, as your Author Count Gabalis*d³* assures us
have a mind to be christened, and since you do me the
Favour to desire a Name from me, take that of Corinna
if you please; I mean not the Lady with whom Ovid was
in Love, but the famous Theban Poetess, who overcame
Pindar five Times, as Historians tell us. I wou'd have
call'd you Sapho, but that I hear you are handsomer.
Since you find I am not altogether a Stranger to you,
be pleased to make me happier by a better Knowledge
of you; and instead of so many unjust Praises which
you give me, think me only worthy of being,

Madam,

Your most humble servant

and Admirer,

John Dryden.

---

*d A new Translation of the entertaining History of the Count de Gabalis,
has been lately printed by E. Curll in the Strand. Price 1s.6d.* [*Footnote in
the 1727 text.*]

Letter 69

DRYDEN TO ELIZABETH THOMAS

Madam,

The great Desire which I observe in you to write well, and those good Parts which God Almighty and Nature have bestowed on you, make me not to doubt that by Application to Study, and the Reading of the best Authors, you may be absolute Mistress of Poetry. 'Tis an unprofitable Art, to those who profess it; but you, who write only for your Diversion, may pass your Hours with Pleasure in it, and without Prejudice, always avoiding (as I know you will) the Licenses which Mrs. Behn allowed herself, of writing loosely, and giving (if I may have leave to say so) some Scandal to the Modesty of her Sex. I confess, I am last Man who ought, in Justice to arraign her, who have been myself too much a Libertine in most of my Poems, which I should be well contented I had Time either to purge or to see them fairly burned.[1] But this I need not say to you, who are too well born, and too well principled, to fall into that Mire.

In the mean Time, I would advise you not to trust too much to Virgil's Pastorals; for as excellent as they are, yet, Theocritus is far before him, both in Softness of Thought, and Simplicity of Expression. Mr.[a] Creech has translated that Greek Poet, which I have not read in English.[2] If you have any considerable

[a] *Mr. Creech's Translation of Theocritus is printed for E. Curll in the Strand, Pr. 2s.6d.* [*Footnote in the 1727 text.*]

Faults, they consist chiefly in the Choice of Words and the placing them so as to make the Verse run smoothly; but I am at present so taken up with my own Studies, that I have not Leisure to descend to Particulars; being in the mean time the fair Corinna's

Most humble and most
faithful Servant,
John Dryden.

P.S. I keep your two[b] Copies till you want them, and are pleased to send for them.

Letter 70

DRYDEN TO MRS. STEWARD

Saturday Nov: 26th

After long Expectation, Madam, at length your happy letter came, to your Servant, who almost despaird of it: The onely comfort I had, was my hopes of seeing you; & that you deferrd writeing, because you wou'd surprise me with your presence, & beare your Relations company to Town. Your Neighbour Mr Price, has given me an Apprehension, that My Cousin your father is in some danger, of being made Sheriff this following yeare; but I hope tis a Jealousy without

---

b *These two Copies of Verses are printed in the Author's Miscellany Poems on several Subjects, for Tho. Combes in Pater-noster-row, 1722. in 8vo. The First is, A Pastoral Elegy, to the Memory of the honourable Cecilia Bew. The Second, The Triple League to Mrs. Susan Dove; written in Imitation of Mrs. Behn* [*Footnote in the 1727 text.*]

ground: And that the warm Season onely keeps him in the Country. If you come up next Week, you will be entertaind with a New Tragedy; which the Author of it, one Mr Dennis, cryes up at an Excessive rate,[1] & Colonel Codrington, who has seen it, prepares the world to give it loud Applauses. Tis calld Iphigenia, & Imi- tated from Eurypides, an old Greek poet. This is to be Acted at Betterton's House, & another play of the same name, is very shortly to come on the stage in Drury Lane.[2] I was lately to visite the Duchess of Norfolk;[3] & she speaks of you with much Affection, & Respect. Your Cousin Montague, after this present Session of Parliament, will be created Earl of Bristoll: &, I hope, is much my friend: But I doubt I am in no Condition of haveing a kindness done me; Haveing the Chancellour my Enemy.[4] And not being capable of re- nounceing the Cause, for which I have so long Sufferd. My Cousin Driden of Chesterton is in Town, & lodges with my Brother in Westminster.[5] My Sonn has seen him, & was very kindly receivd by him. Let this Let- ter stand for nothing, because it has nothing[a] but news in it; & has so little of the main business, wch is to assure my fair Cousine, how much I am her Admirer, & her most devoted Servant,

John Dryden.

I write no Recommendations of Service to our friends at Oundle, because I suppose they are leaveing that place. But I wish my Cousin Stuart a Boy, as like Miss Jem:[6] as He & you can make him. My wife and

[a] of *lined through immediately after* nothing

Sonn, are never forgetfull of their Acknowledgments
to you both.

For Mrs Stuart, Att
Cotterstock near Oundle
In the County of Northton
These
To be left at the Posthouse
In Oundle.

Letter 71

DRYDEN TO MRS. STEWARD

Thursday, Dec: the 14th-99.

Madam
        When I have either too much business, or want
health to write*a* to you, I count my time is lost, or at
Least my Conscience accuses me that I spend it ill: At
this time my head is full of cares; and my body ill at
ease. My Book[1] is printing, & my Bookseller makes no
hast. I had last night at bed time, an unwelcome fit of
vomiting; & my Sonn Charles lyes sick upon his bed*b*
with the Colique: which has been violent upon him, for
almost a week. with all this, I cannot but remember,
that you accusd me of barbarity, I hope, in jeast onely,
for mistaking one Sheriff for another,[2] which proceeded
from my want of heareing well. I am heartily sorry
that a chargeable office is fallen on my Cousin Stuart.

a to write *is repeated, and the second is lined through*
b Bed *written between the lines*

But my Cousin Driden comforts me, that it must have come one time or other, like the Smallpox; & better to have it young than old. I hope it will[c] leave no great marks behind it, & that your fortune will no more feel it, than your beauty, by the addition of a years wearing: My cousine your mother, was heer yesterday, to see my wife, though I had not the happiness to be at home. Both the Iphiginias[3] have been playd with bad Success; & being both acted, one against the other, in the same week, clashd together, like two rotten ships, which cou'd not endure the shock; & sunk to rights. The King's Proclamation against vice and profaneness is issued out in print: but a deep disease is not to be cur'd with a slight Medicine.[4] The parsons who must read it, will find as little effect from it, as from their dull Sermons: tis a Scare-Crow, w[ch] will not fright many birds from preying on the fields & orchards. The best News I heare, is, that the Land, will not be chargd very deep this yeare:[5] let that comfort you for your Shriev-alty; & continue me in your good graces, who am, fair Cousine

Your most faithfull, obligd Servant

John Dryden.

For Mrs Stuart, Att
Cotterstock, near Oundle
In Northamptonshyre
These,
To be left with the Postmaster
of Oundle.

---

[c] will *written between the lines*

Letter 72

DRYDEN TO ELIZABETH THOMAS

Fair Ccrinna,

I have sent your Poems back again, after having kept them so long from you: By which you see I am like the rest of the World, an impudent Borrower, and a bad Pay-master. You take more Care of my Health than it deserves; that of an old Man is always crazy, and at present, mine is worse than usual, by a St. Anthony's Fire[1] in one of my legs; tho' the Swelling is much abated, yet the Pain is not wholly gone, and I am too weak to stand upon it. If I recover, it is possible I may attempt Homer's Iliads: A Specimen of it (the first Book) is now in the Press, among other Poems of mine, which will make a[a] Volume in Folio, of twelve Shillings Price; and will be published within this Month.[2] I desire, fair Author, that you will be pleased to continue me in your good Graces, who am with all Sincerity and Gratitude,

Your most humble
Servant, and Admirer,
John Dryden.

Friday, December
29th. 1699.

---

[a] *The Volume here referred to by Mr. Dryden, is (what commonly goes by the Title) of his Fables, &c.* [*Footnote in the 1727 text.*]

Letter 73

DRYDEN TO MRS. STEWARD

Feb. 23d

Madam,

Though I have not leisure to thank you for the last trouble I gave you, yet haveing by me two lampoons lately made, I know not but they may be worth your reading; and therefore have presum'd to send them. I know not the authours; but the Town will be ghessing. The Ballad of The Pews, which are lately rais'd higher at St. James's church, is by some sayd to be Mr. Manwairing, or my Lord Peterborough: the Poem of The Confederates some think to be Mr. Walsh:[1] the copies are both lik'd. And there are really two factions of ladyes, for the two play-houses. If you do not understand the names of some persons mention'd I can help you to the knowledge of them. You know, Sir Tho: Skipwith[2] is master of the play-house in Drury-Lane; and my Lord Scarsdale[3] is the patron of Betterton's house, being in love with somebody there. The Lord Scott is second sonn to the Duchess of Monmouth. I need not tell you who my Lady Darentwater is;[4] but it may be you know not her lord is a poet, and none of the best.[5] Forgive this hasty billet, from

Your most oblig'd Servant.,
John Dryden.

For Mrs. Stewart,
Att Cotterstock near Oundle,
in Northamptonshyre,
These.
To be left with the Postmaster
of Oundle.

Letter 74

DRYDEN TO MRS. STEWARD

Tuesday March the 12th 1699 [/1700]

Madam

Tis a week since I receivd the favour of a letter, which I have not yet Acknowledgd to you. About that time, my new Poems were publish'd; which are not come till this day into my hands. They are a debt to you I must Confess, and I am glad, because^a they are so Unworthy to be made a Present. Your Sisters I hope, will be so kind to have them convey'd to you; that my writeings may have the honour of waiting on you, which is denyd to me. The Town encourages them with more Applause than any thing of mine deserves; And particularly My Cousin Driden[1] accepted One from me so very Indulgently, that it makes me more & more in Love with him. But all Our hopes of the House of Commons, are wholly dashd; Our Proprieties are destroyd: and rather than we shoud not perish, they have made a breach in the Magna Charta; for which God forgive them.[2] Congreves New Play[3] has had but moderate success; though it deserves much better. I am neither in health, nor do I want Afflictions of any kind; but am in all Conditions, Madam, Your most Obligd, Obedient Servant,

John Dryden.

Ffor Mrs Stuart,
Att Cotterstock near Oundle,
These.
By the Oundle Carrier, with
A Book, directed to her
Northamptonshyre, These.

^a because *written between the lines*

Letter 75

DRYDEN TO MRS. STEWARD

Madam

The Ladies of the Town have infected you at a distance: they are all of your Opinion; & like my last Book of Poems, better than any thing they have formerly seen of mine. I always thought my Verses to my Cousin Driden were the best of the whole; & to my comfort the Town thinks them so; & He, which pleases me most is of the same Judgment as appears by a noble present he has sent me, which surprisd me, because I did not in the least expect it. I doubt not but He receivd what you were pleasd to send him; because He sent me the Letter, which you did me the favour to write me. At this very Instant I heare the Guns, which goeing off, give me to understand that the King is goeing to the Parliament, to pass Acts; & Consequently to prorogue them: for yesterday I heard, that both He & the*a* Lords have given up the Cause; & the House of Commons have gaind an Entire victory; though, under the Rose, I am of Opinion, that much of the Confidence is abated on either side; & that whensoever they meet next, it will give that House a farther occasion, of encroaching on the prerogative & the Lords. for they who beare the purse will rule. The Parliament being risen My Cousin Driden will immediately be with you, & I believe, return his thanks in person. All this while I am lame at home; & have not stirrd abroad

a the *written between the lines*

this Moneth at least: Neither my wife nor Charles are well. but have intrusted their Service in my hand. I humbly add my own to the Unwilling High Sheriff, & wish him fairly at an end of his trouble. The latter end of last week, I had the honour of a visite from my Cousine your mother, & my Cousine Dorothy, with which I was much comforted: Within this moneth there will be playd for my profit, an old play of Fletchers, calld the Pilgrim, corrected by my good friend Mr Vanbrook;[1] to which I have added A New Masque, & am to write a New Prologue & Epilogue.[2] Southerns tragedy, calld the Revolt of Capoua,[3] will be playd At Bettertons House within this fortnight. I am out with that Company, & therefore if I can help it, will not read it before tis Acted; though the Authour much desires I shou'd.[4] do not think I will refuse a present from fair hands; for I am resolvd to save my Bacon. I beg your pardon, for this slovenly letter; but I have not health to transcribe it. My Service to my Cousin your Brother, who I heare is happy in your Company, which He is not, who most desires it, & who is, Madam,

Your most obligd, Obedient Servant
John Dryden.

Thursday, April the 11th
1700.

For Mrs Stuart, Att
Cotterstock, neare Oundle in
Northamptonshyre,
These
To be left with the
postmaster of Oundle.

Letter 76

RICHARD SWAN TO DRYDEN

Sir,

When I saw you last, you gave me your *Word* that you would send me a Pound of Snuff in two Days Time; but what signifies your *Word*; for if you had kept your *Word*, I had had it long a go. Now, though you left your *Word* with me, I don't know what to do with it; I am afraid nobody will take your *Word* (I mean for a Pound of Snuff) unless you retrieve it very soon. But it may be you only designed a Compliment to my Understanding, believing I knew you so well, as not to depend upon your *Word*, for *Words* are but Wind, and so indeed a *Word* to the Wise is sufficient.

However, you will find if you continue thus to forfeit your *Word*, that your *Word*, by the Bye, will become a *Bye-Word*; nevertheless, something may be said in Favour of your *Word*; as for Example; that though it brought me not a Pound of Snuff, and consequently proved a *Word* of no Weight, yet it is certain, that I have taken Snuff at it in some measure.

Perhaps you will not like my Quibbling, because it is playing upon a *Word*; but, when your *Word* ceases to pass in earnest, then it naturally passes into a Jest, and so in a *Word*, your *Word* is the Occasion of these *Words* I've wrote, and of so many *Words* more which I have still to say, when I have a farther Opportunity of *wording* on't with you by *Word* of Mouth, which shall be next Time we meet upon the *Word* of

Your humble Servant,
Richard Swan

Letter 77

CHARLES GILDON TO DRYDEN

May the 10th. 1693

I hope, Sir, you'd not measure my Love and Value for you by the Visits I make you, for then you wou'd extreamly injure me; for I cannot be so impudent with a man I have an aweful Esteam for, as to intrude too often into his Company, for I'm sensible I can in no measure attone for the loss of that time, my Visits wou'd rob from your better Thoughts; and I rather satisfie my self with the expression of my Zeal and Love in absence, than, at the expence of my Friend, gratifie my own desire of his frequent Company. But yet, I confess, this long default of my Duty can be excus'd by nothing but the unavoidable business about my Concerns in the Country, which has divorc'd me as long from, what I value next to you, my Books.

Mistake me not, Sir, I mean not my Scribling, which I'm far enough from valuing, and only comply with, by the compelling Obligation that taught the Parrot, suum XAIPE. Nay, I have so little of an Author, that I have not Arrogance, and want all Self-Esteem, which some ev'n as dull as my self abound with beyond bearing; and which is, indeed, like a Wife, tho' an Evil, yet such a one that is necessary. For a Diffidence of one's self in Writing, as well as in Addresses to the Fair and the Great, is seldom any advantage to a Man, at least in this Age, where the highest Impudence passes for a handsom Assurance, and Noise and much Talk for

Wit, and Repartée: It dispirits a Man, and he can't please himself with what he Writes, so he very hardly can rise to the tast of any that are not duller. But when I was forc'd to this Curse of Scribling, I furnish'd my self with as much of a Stoic, as I cou'd, to fortifie my self against publick Censure; and in my own defence soon believ'd Reputation but a Whim, since the Worst had their Admirers, as well as the Best, at least in our Age; nor cou'd I perswade my self that the next wou'd be one jot better in its Judgment. And to say truth, there is nothing cou'd make me have any tolerable Opinion of my self, but the Love and Esteem I have for you; whom (give me leave to contradict my self, and shew such Arrogance) I do pretend to value, as much as any Man can: and I defie my greatest Enemies to do me Justice, and contradict me by any word or discourse ev'n where I had a Moral Certainty, you cou'd never hear of it again.

This, Sir, I urge, as a Praise of my self; for next to being a good Poet, is to know how to value one; the first has given Immortality, the latter (when in a Man of Quality) gain'd it. But lest the lenght of my Letter shou'd do, what I apprehend from my Visits I'll
Subscribe my self,
Your Friend and humble Servant
Charles Gildon

NOTES

NOTES

The Frontispiece

This portrait of Dryden, now in the possession of Percy Dryden Mundy, Esq., of Great Chesterford, Essex, has not hitherto been reproduced. It is presumably by Kneller, and undoubtedly that described by Bell as being then in the possession of Charles Beville Dryden (*The Poetical Works of John Dryden*, I, 98): "The picture is a half-length, in a court costume of French grey silk, with gold ornamental studs instead of buttons, laced cravat, and plain ruffles at the wrist, a wig and sword, and a wreath of laurel in the left hand."

Letter 1 . . . page 3

In the William Andrews Clark Memorial Library, Los Angeles. It was first printed by Malone, who after examining the defaced original with a "microscope," dated it May 23, 1655. No figures are now visible, so that any date must be conjectural. Since it is dated at Cambridge, Dryden was presumably still at Trinity College. When he finally left college is uncertain, though Christie in the introduction to the Globe Edition of the *Select Poems of John Dryden* and in a communication to *Notes and Queries*, 4th ser., X, 370 (Nov. 9, 1872), presents evidence which suggests that Dryden had left before May, 1655. Dryden, it should be recalled, had taken his B.A. in January, 1653/4; and there is no reason to believe that he was in residence after that time. I am inclined therefore to date the letter 1653.

Honor Dryden was the poet's cousin, a daughter of Sir John Driden of Canons Ashby. Bell (*op. cit.*, I, 18-19) prints several of her letters which he found at Canons Ashby, and one of her sister Ann's, in which is mentioned a "Mr. Conseat." This person, according to Bell, may have been the poet. There is no evidence whatever for such an identification, or for the romance between Honor and Dryden which he suggests.

1. The Reverend Levite was perhaps a fellow student whom Dryden used on this occasion as a messenger to carry his letter. There is no hint here or elsewhere of his identity.

2. This may be merely a phrase, or it may mean that Dryden continued at Cambridge the writing of poetry which he had begun at Westminster. There are no extant poems of the Cambridge period.

Letter 2 . . . page 5

James M. Osborn prints it and describes the circumstances mentioned in it in *John Dryden: Some Biographical Facts and Problems* (New York, 1940), pp. 255 ff. The date is that written on the outside of the sheet by Richard Salwey.

1. He was Edward Salwey, son of Dorothy Dryden, Dryden's aunt.

2. According to the notations of Richard Salwey on the letter, Edward indicated his desire to leave all to him, rather than to his own sisters. No will was made, however, and the estate passed to his sisters upon his death.

Letter 3 . . . page 6

In the *Alfred Morrison Collection*, ed. A. W. Thibaudeau, p. 47, plate 67. It has been reproduced in facsimile in *Die Englische Literatur von der Renaissance bis zur Aufklärung*, by Wolfgang Keller and Bernhard Fehr (Potsdam, 1928), p. 180. It is undoubtedly written from the seat of the Earl of Berkshire at Charlton, Wiltshire, where Dryden had retired during the plague. At this time Sir Robert Long was Chancellor of the Exchequer, and a colleague of Sir Robert Howard, Dryden's brother-in-law.

1. The patent referred to is that of £3,000, which had been granted to Lady Elizabeth Howard in 1662, apparently on the assignment of the Earl of Berkshire, her father. It was to be paid out of the revenue of the Excise at the rate of £250 a quarter (*Cal. State Papers, Domestic, 1661-2,* p. 288). For a discussion of this grant and its payment, see my article, "A Biographical Note on John Dryden," *Modern Language Review*, XXVII (1932), 206-210. It would appear from Dryden's words that Sir Robert Long had been the intermediary in the original assignment. Though evidence is lacking, I suggest that the patent for £3,000, made over to Lady Elizabeth in 1662, was in the nature of a dowry which she was to bring to Dryden. They were married at St. Swithin's on December 1, 1663. See Bell, *op. cit.,* I, 24.

2. The "unreasonable proposition" we can only guess at. None of the £3,000 had been paid before June, 1666, two months before the date of this letter. Perhaps Dryden's father-in-law had reconsidered, and was seeking a portion of the expected payments for himself.

3. This letter, formerly in the possession of Mr. Percy J. Dobell, is now in the Folger Shakespeare Library, which has furnished me a photostatic copy. Dated at Vasterne [Hampshire], August 13, 1666, it is as follows:

Sr

You will receive with this an enclos'd acquittance signed by Mr Driden and his wife my sister; for seaven hundred sixty eight pounds fifteen shillings wch Mr Sheppeard sent downe to be signd: I beinge entrusted by them both; due desire that you will be pleasd S^r to receive the mony that shall be paid upon it; and allow Mr Sheppeard such deductions and charges as he shall reasonably demand; and this to keepe in your hand's till farther order from them and

> Y^or most faithfull
> friend & humble
> Servant
> Ro: Howard

S^r

> pray if Mr Sheppeard need's
> your assistance in any thinge
> be pleasd to afford it for wee
> apprehend some stop because
> my Lord Ushley is out of towne.

Letter 4 . . . page 7

In the British Museum, Harl. 7003, f. 293-5. Malone first printed the letter, and dated it July, 1673, but in my opinion this is at least two—possibly three—months late. Dryden mentions the Dedication to Rochester of *Marriage à la Mode*. The play was registered in S.R. on March 18, and Herringman's advertisement for the printed play appeared in the *London Gazette*, No. 786, May 29-June 2. Furthermore, Dryden refers to the fact that the Duke of B[uckingham] is "pursuing the honour of Lieutenant General which flyes him." Buckingham was finally appointed to this rank on May 13 (*Cal. State Papers, Dom., 1673*, p. 242). Therefore the letter must be dated near the first of May or before. Rochester was well disposed toward Dryden, as indeed this letter suggests; but within a few years, the friendship had turned to enmity. The reasons for Rochester's change are far from clear, though possibly the Earl of Mulgrave's patronage of Dryden, from 1674 or 1675 onwards, contributed to Rochester's disaffection. No careful study of the relationship between the two men at this time is available; but for the feud see Johannes Prinz, *John Wilmot, Earl of Rochester* (Leipzig, 1927), and V. de Sola Pinto, *Rochester* (London, 1935).

1. Dryden refers to his dedication to Rochester of *Marriage à la Mode*, which was registered on March 18 as *Amorous Adventures, or Marriage à la Mode*. It had probably been acted before the end of 1671. See my article, "The Dates of Two Dryden Plays," *Publications of the Modern Language Association*, LI (1936), 786-792.

2. When Dryden says "you are that Rerum Natura of your own Lucretius," he refers to Rochester's translation of Lucretius, II, 646-651, which is printed as follows in John Hayward's *Collected Works of John Wilmot, Earl of Rochester* (London, 1926), p. 45:

> The Gods, by right of Nature, must possess
> An everlasting Age of perfect Peace:
> Far off remov'd from us and our affairs;
> Neither approach'd by Dangers, or by Cares:
> Rich in themselves, to whom we cannot add:
> Not pleas'd by Good Deeds; nor provok'd by Bad.

3. The first Duke of Buckingham set off on a disastrous expedition to the Low Countries on June 27, 1627. On July 10, with a hundred ships and six thousand men, he was at the Isle of Rhé; on the twelfth he began the siege of St. Martin's fortress. He was ignominiously defeated.

4. In this, the only personal and private comment of the poet on Villiers, it is interesting to recognize the seeds of the famous character of Zimri in *Absalom and Achitophel*, eight years later.

5. "That dangerous part of wit" Dryden may have indeed forsworn. At the time this letter was written, the satires, some of them on Dryden, known under the general title of *Censure of the Rota*, were appearing. Dryden's comment on satire may have been provoked by this series. For a list of the separate titles see Macdonald, *Bibliography of John Dryden*, pp. 201 ff.

6. The reference here is to Boileau's *Satire*, I, ll. 51-54:

> Je ne puis rien nommer, si ce n'est par son nom,
> J'appelle un chat un chat, et Rolet un fripon,
> De servir un Amant, je n'en ai pas l'adresse.

The verses of Etherege apparently died in manuscript, for they are not to be found among his extant work.

7. Malone (I, ii, p. 9) identifies him with Sir John Eaton, a writer of songs.

8. Tregonwell Frampton (1641-1727), a well-known gambler.

9. "Brother John" I have been unable to identify.

10. This was probably Robert Constable, third Viscount of Dunbar. On May 3, 1671, he pleaded guilty at the Old Bailey to a charge of murdering one Peter Varnall, by stabbing him in the head with a rapier. Before he came up for trial, he had obtained the king's pardon (*Complete Peerage*, V. Gibbs).

11. Henry Brounckard was a Gentleman of the Bed Chamber to the Duke of York, and a gambler of some reputation.

12. Aubrey de Vere, the 20th Earl of Oxford, was one of the profligate young lords who scandalized the town after the Restoration.

Like some of his betters, he found at the playhouse a mistress, Elizabeth Davenport, who bore him a son in 1664. See Pepys's *Diary, passim*.

13. The King's Players at Oxford have been the subject of considerable interest; but little is known of the date of the performance here alluded to. See the correspondence in the *Times Literary Supplement* for February 21, 28, March 14, April 11, 25, May 2, 1929, and January 16, 1930.

The prologue and epilogue were first printed in *Miscellany Poems* (1684). In the epilogue Dryden mentions the "plagues of French Comedians and Italian Merry-Andrews on the English stage." The French troupe came over in December, 1672, and were followed in April, 1673, by the Italian players (*Cal. Treasury Books, 1672-75*, pp. 14, 119).

14. Rochester was possibly at Woodstock, or Adderbury, in Oxfordshire. When Dryden says "four-score" miles, he may be speaking loosely; both of these places are closer to London. Rochester was Keeper of the Lodge at Woodstock; his estate was at Adderbury.

Letter 5 . . . page 11

In the collection of the Historical Society of Pennsylvania, Philadelphia. It is addressed probably to Edward Osborne, Lord Latimer (1655-1689), son of the Earl of Danby. The title Viscount Latimer was a courtesy title which the son held from 1674 to his death. He was a Gentleman of the Bed Chamber to Charles II. Although it has long been known that Dryden's range of acquaintances was large, no one has heretofore been aware of this new friend, Latimer. The connection, indeed, is a bit puzzling; for Latimer at twenty-two years of age, and quite undistinguished, seems at this distance to have been hardly the kind of patron Dryden could be interested in. It may well prove, as several sentences in the letter suggest, that Dryden was using the young man as an approach to his father, Danby.

Though undated, there is enough internal evidence to place it in July, 1677. See the notes below. I published it in the *Times Literary Supplement*, October 29, 1938.

1. This was probably Robert Bertie, third Earl of Lindsey. He was elected F.R.S. in 1666, and in March, 1673/4, was appointed a Gentleman of the Bed Chamber to the King, in the Duke of Buckingham's place (*Hist. MSS. Comm. 7th Report*, p. 491). No evidence exists to show that Dryden was helped by Lindsey; indeed, their names have not hitherto been linked. The only certain connection between Dryden and the Bertie family is that of his poem "Eleonora," written years later in honor of the deceased wife of James Bertie, Earl of Abdingdon, with whom he admitted he was unacquainted.

2. Dryden refers undoubtedly to *Mr. Limberham, or The Kind Keeper*, which was finally acted in March, 1677/8. The King's collaboration with Dryden quite possibly amounted to no more than furnishing an episode for one part of the comedy. The history of the presentation of *Limberham* suggests that the King did not "keep the jeast in countenance"; for it was taken from the stage, after three nights, by royal command. The acting version probably contained some cutting satire upon a powerful figure in the Court, who made representations and forced its early demise. For support of this suggestion, see Dryden's Preface to the printed play. D'Urfey's *A Fond Husband* had appeared in May, 1676.

3. The request seems to have been successful; for on July 31 letters patent were issued, granting Dryden an additional pension of £100. For a survey of the pension payments and the financial arrangements, see L. I. Bredvold, "Notes on John Dryden's Pension," *Modern Philology*, XXX (1933), 267-274, and the present writer's "A Biographical Note on John Dryden," *Modern Language Review*, XXVII (1932), 206-210.

4. John Sheffield, Earl of Mulgrave, became Dryden's patron about 1674. In 1676 Dryden dedicated to him the play *Aureng-Zebe*. In the dedicatory epistle he recalls Mulgrave's offices as intermediary between the King and him, and also the plan of the proposed epic, which was languishing because of the King's lack of interest. Mulgrave continued to be a patron of the poet until Dryden's death.

5. Who Mr. Mayes was and what this persecution was, can only be guessed at. Perhaps the reference is to Baptist May, Charles's Keeper of the Privy Purse, for Dryden's complaint seems to refer to money matters. The Keeper could doubtless have obstructed or delayed payments to the poet laureate.

6. The play is of course *All for Love*. It was finally on the stage in December, 1677. It was registered in S.R. on January 31, 1677/8, and published in March, as appears from the advertisement in the *London Gazette*, March 21-25, 1678. The permission to dedicate to Danby, as requested in the letter, was granted.

Letter 6 . . . page 13

Now in the R. B. Adam Johnsonian Library, University of Rochester. It was printed and reproduced in facsimile in the *Catalog of the R. B. Adam Library* (New York, 1929), III, 87-88. The letter is undated and unaddressed. The mention of Rymer's *Tragedies of the Last Age* helps to set a reasonably accurate date, for this book had appeared in the late summer of 1677. In a letter to Mulgrave dated August 20, Wycherley says that Dryden is in Northamptonshire and mentions Rymer's book as recently published. This letter, therefore, dates in the late summer or early autumn. Dorset is the person addressed; he was possessed of estates in Northamptonshire, whence the letter came. See James M. Osborn, *op. cit.*, p. 264, for a discussion of the case for Dorset as the recipient.

1. In later years Dryden's visits in the country were spent at Oundle or Tichmarsh. Whether he was now at either of these villages or elsewhere is uncertain. See note 2.

2. Miss B. Trissham (Tresham) was probably a daughter of the George Tresham who held the manor of Pilton in 1677, and who died in 1684. Dryden may have been staying at Lilford, for Pilton Manor would have been only about a half-mile distant. (See *Victoria County History, Northamptonshire*, III, 130.)

3. The "wise cousin" I have been unable to identify. It may have been Mr. Elmes, from whose house the carrier was to leave.

4. For a discussion of Dryden's critical answer to the book, see Fred G. Walcott, "John Dryden's Answer to Thomas Rymer's *The Tragedies of the Last Age*," *Philological Quarterly*, XV (1936), 194-214.

5. Rymer's *Edgar*, unacted, was published in the late autumn or winter. It was advertised in the *London Gazette* for January 14-17, 1677/8. See Sybil Rosenfeld, "Dramatic Advertisements in the Burney Newspapers 1660-1700," *Publications of the Modern Language Association*, LI (1936), 123-152.

Letter 7 . . . page 14

In the collection of the Marquess of Crewe, through whose kindness I am able to print the authentic text. It was first printed by Scott in 1808.

1. These verses, upon which Dryden is pronouncing judgment, are translated from Lucretius, *De Rerum Natura*, I, 225-228. A modern translation by W. H. D. Rouse, in the Loeb Classical Library, is: "Besides, if time consuming all the material utterly destroys whatever by lapse of years it removes, whence does Venus restore living creatures to the light of life each after its kind." Creech's translation (ll. 270-273 in the 1714 ed.) follows:

> If all Things, over which long Years prevail,
> Did wholly perish, and their Matter fail,
> How could the Pow'rs of all-kind Venus breed
> A constant Race of An'mals to succeed. . . .

2. Thomas Creech (1659-1700) took his B.A. at Wadham College in 1680. Two years later he brought out his *Lucretius*, which went into a second edition in 1683, and which remains his literary monument. Encouraged by the reception of the *Lucretius*, Creech published in 1684

The Odes, Satyrs, and Epistles of Horace, which he dedicated to Dryden. In 1700, disappointed in love and beset by financial difficulties, he committed suicide.

Letter 8 . . . page 17

In the William Andrews Clark Memorial Library. Though the letter is undated, Malone, who first published it, conjectured, no doubt correctly, that it was written in 1682. Richard Busby was the great, and proverbially severe, master of Westminster school from 1640 until his death in 1695. During his incumbency, he produced a host of successful men. Dryden was under him until 1650, when he was elected to Trinity College, Cambridge. In 1693 he inscribed the translation of the fifth Satire of Persius to Busby. For a sympathetic account of Busby, see G. F. Russell Barker's *Memoir of Richard Busby, with some account of Westminster School in the Seventeenth Century* (London, 1895).

The following letter from Lady Elizabeth Dryden to Busby was printed by Malone, I, ii, 14-15. As he pointed out, it appears to have been written at about the same time as Dryden's letters to Busby. I do not know the provenience of his text, which I follow; nor do I know the present whereabouts of the letter, if indeed it is extant.

Honnored Sir,   Ascension Day [1682?]

I hope I need use noe other argument to you in excuse of my sonn for not coming to church to Westminster then this, that he now lies at home, and thearfore cannot esilly goe soe far backwards and forwards. His father and I will take care that he shall duely goe to church heare, both on holydayes and Sundays, till he comes to be more nearly under your care in the college. In the mean time, will you pleas to give me leave to accuse you of forgetting your prommis conserning my eldest sonn; who, as you once assured me, was to have one night in a weeke alowed him to be at home, in considirasion both of his health and cleanliness. You know, Sir, that prommises mayd to women, and espiceally mothers, will never faill to bee cald upon, and thearfore I will add noe more but that I am, at this time, your remembrancer, and allwayes, Honnord Sir,

                                  Your humble Servant,
                                  E. Dryden.

1. The younger son is John Dryden, Jr.; the elder, Charles, who had entered Westminster in 1680. John—though the record is none too clear—must have entered in the summer of 1682. He was thus in his first term. See Joseph Welch, *A List of the Queen's Scholars of St. Peter's College, Westminster* (London, 1852), pp. 185, 194, 199, 203; and G. F. R. Barker and A. H. Stenning, *The Record of Old Westminsters*, I, 288-289.

Letter 9 . . . page 18

In the Harvard College Library. It was first printed by Malone. Though undated, it must have been written in 1682, since both of the boys were at Westminster.

1. Charles's dismissal was apparently only a temporary suspension; for he was elected to Trinity College, Cambridge, where he was admitted pensioner on June 26, 1683 (Barker and Stenning, *op. cit.*, I, 288).

2. I am unable to identify Mr. Meredith.

3. Malone explains *Custos* as follows (I, ii, 16) : "In the hall of the College of Westminster, when the boys are at dinner, it is *ex officio* the place of the second boy in the second election to keep order among the two under elections; and if any word, after he has ordered silence, be spoken, except in Latin, he says to the speaker, tu es custos; and this term passes from the second speaker to the third or more, till dinner is over. Whoever is then *Custos*, has an imposition [i.e., a fine]."

4. Dr. John Dolben, who became Archbishop of York in August, 1683.

5. As Malone pointed out, this person was named Robert Morgan. He had entered Westminster with Charles, as a King's Scholar, in 1680. He was elected to Christ Church, Oxford, in 1682 and matriculated on December 14, 1682, aged seventeen years (Barker and Stenning, *op. cit.*, II, 664).

Letter 10 . . . page 20

In the British Museum, Add. MS. 17017. It was first printed by Malone. Though unaddressed, I believe, as tradition holds, that it was written to Lawrence Hyde, the second son of Lord Chancellor Clarendon. He had been created Earl of Rochester in 1682. Early in 1683 Dryden dedicated to him *The Duke of Guise*, and nine years later, *Cleomenes*. At this time Rochester was first Lord of the Treasury.

The letter is undated. Malone conjectures August, 1683, and I am inclined to think that this is fairly close, but not for Malone's reasons. In the first sentence Dryden mentions Sunderland's intercession on his behalf for a half-year's salary. In this year Dryden seems to have been on friendly terms with Sunderland; for Evelyn records in his *Diary* under date of June 17, 1683: "I dined at the Earl of Sunderland's with the Earls of Bath, Castlehaven, Lords Viscounts Falconberg, Falkland, Bishop of London, The Grand Master of Malta, brother to the Duke of Vendôme (a young wild spark), and Mr. Dryden, the poet." Furthermore, on August 22, 1683, Dryden was granted a payment of £75 on his pension—which may have been a partial answer to his plea. See my article, "A Biographical Note on John Dryden," *Modern Language Review*, XXVII (1932), 206-210.

1. Jesuites powder: quinine.

2. Dryden's comment here suggests that after his satires in 1681 and 1682 the Whigs had attempted to bribe him to their support. There is, so far as I know, absolutely no corroboration for such suggestion. What his "beneficiall studies" were I am not sure. He may refer to preliminary studies for the opera which a year later was being rehearsed in its truncated form—*Albion and Albanius*. Or he may refer to the studies for the translation of *The History of the League*. Of the two I prefer the second conjecture. See the notes below.

3. The Earl of Clarendon, Lord Chancellor until 1667, when he was banished through the efforts of his enemies. It is possible that Dryden refers to his verses "To My Lord Chancellor," written in 1662. But it seems more reasonable to believe that he alludes to a work or a tribute, now unknown, written between 1674 and 1683. Clarendon died in 1674.

4. The eldest sons have been noted above. The third son, Erasmus Henry, was elected to Charterhouse in September, 1682, on the recommendation of the King, in preference to two other boys. For the petitions of William Levett and Henry Kramer, with the King's answer, regarding the preference shown the poet's son, see the *Cal. State Papers, Domestic, January 1-December 31, 1682*, pp. 435-436; and *January 1-June 30, 1683*, p. 33.

5. This was the Duke of York, afterwards James II. In 1667 Dryden had dedicated *Annus Mirabilis* to him.

6. He was not appointed Collector of the Customs. See my note, "Was John Dryden Collector of Customs?" *Modern Language Notes*, XLVII (1932), 246-249, and L. I. Bredvold, "Notes on John Dryden's Pension," *Modern Philology*, XXX (1933), 267-274.

7. Although there is no definite evidence to identify the work mentioned here, it was very likely Dryden's translation of Maimbourg's *The History of the League*, which was registered in S.R. on April 2, 1684, advertised as in the press on April 16, in the *Observator*, II, No. 45, and published the last of July (the *London Gazette*, No. 1951, July 28-31, 1684). In dedicating the book to the King, he mentions the fact that Charles had commanded the translation.

Letter 11 . . . page 22

In the British Museum, Egerton MS. 2869, f. 30. It was first printed by Malone. His date—September, 1684—may be a month late. Since the *History of the League* was published at the end of July, the public comment on the book might reasonably be expected in August. The letter is written from Northamptonshire.

1. Probably, as Malone suggests, because of the death of his wife, which occurred on July 21.

2. The Earl of Roscommon's *Essay on Translated Verse* was reprinted. The second edition bears the date 1685, though it probably appeared in the late autumn of 1684. Dryden's verse was corrected according to his instructions.

3. This refers to Charles Dryden's Latin verses prefixed to Roscommon's poem.

4. This was Knightley Chetwood, a friend of both Dryden and Roscommon. He wrote a life of the latter, a copy of which is now among the Baker MSS. See Carl Niemeyer in *Modern Language Notes*, XLIX (1934), 432-437. In 1692 Chetwood contributed a "Character" of St. Evremond, which was continued and completed by Dryden, and prefixed to the edition in that year of *Miscellaneous Essays*. In 1697 he contributed a life of Vergil and a preface to the *Pastorals* for Dryden's *Virgil*.

5. The Miscellanies referred to here is probably *Sylvae, or the Second Part of Poetical Miscellanies*, S.R., January 10, 1685; advertised in the *Observator* for January 1, 1685. See Macdonald, *Bibliography*, p. 71. Dryden apparently had planned to include the *Religio Laici* in these miscellanies, but as suggested here was dissuaded by Tonson in the interest of a completely new volume.

6. To *Sylvae*, Dryden contributed considerably more than he suggests here. From Horace were included the ninth ode of the first book, the twenty-ninth ode of the third book (inscribed to the Earl of Rochester), the third ode of the first book, and the second epode. Instead of forty lines from Lucretius, he translated about sixty lines from the beginning of the first book, the beginning of the second (about seventy lines), three hundred and twenty-one lines from the latter part of the third book, nearly three hundred lines from the fourth book, and a few lines from the fifth. The story of Nisus and Euryalus was included, as well as Theocritus's eighteenth, twenty-third, and twenty-seventh Idyls.

7. The opera was, I believe, *Albion and Albanius*, which appears to have been two-thirds completed at this time. In the preface to the published work in the following summer, Dryden says that the King had been pleased "twice or thrice to command that it should be practiced before him, especially the first and third acts of it." Public presentation was expected in the early weeks of January; for in a letter to the Countess of Rutland, dated January 1, Edward Bedingfield writes: "Wee are in expectation of an opera composed by Mr. Dryden, and set by Grabuche [Grabu], and so well performed at the Duchess of Portsmouth's, pleaseth mightily, but the rates proposed will not take soe well, for they have set the boxes at a guyny a place, and the Pitt at halfe.

They advance 4000 £ on the opera" (*Hist. MSS. Comm., Rutland,* II, 85).

8. I cannot identify this man. He may have been a tradesman.

9. The "singing opera" is obviously not *Albion*. Although I am not sure what it is, I believe it may be Dryden and D'Avenant's *Tempest*, with the songs performed by professional singers. See E. J. Dent, *Foundations of English Opera* (Cambridge, 1928), p. 216.

10. *All for Love* and *The Conquest of Granada*.

11. Charlotte Butler was one of the best singers and actresses on the stage at this time. She performed in *Calisto* in 1674 (Allardyce Nicoll, *A History of Restoration Drama*, p. 321) and later made a success in Betterton's opera *The Prophetess* and in Dryden's *King Arthur*. Octavia is of course Antony's wife in *All for Love*.

12. This is probably Sarah Cooke, a member of Betterton's company.

13. Susanna (Sue) Percival first married the actor William Mountford, and later, Verbruggen. As Mrs. Verbruggen she was a famous actress after the turn of the century. Benzayda is one of the lovers in *The Conquest of Granada*.

14. John, his second son.

Letter 12 . . . page 25

In the Bodleian, MS. Malone 9, f. 70b. It was first printed in the *Bodleian Quarterly Record*, VII, No. 84 (1934), pp. 503 ff., by Miss Phillis Freeman. Like most of the Walsh letters it is undated and unsigned. The date of composition of the letter as assigned by Miss Freeman—1686—I am prepared to accept; for there is no reason to dispute her dating of MS. Malone 9 in that year. This letter, however, is a rough draft, and like the other Walsh letters was probably not dispatched in such a crude form. My guess is that it was not posted in 1686, but in 1690. See Letter 15, below, which appears to be the answer to this first letter from Walsh.

William Walsh (1663-1708) was a native of Worcestershire. He was educated at Wadham College, and early made the acquaintance of Dryden, who, along with others, thought highly of Walsh's abilities as a poet and critic. His *Dialogue Concerning Women* appeared as his first published work in 1691. In the following year he published a small book of poems and letters. In the course of his literary career he became a friend of Pope, Wycherley, Congreve, and Vanbrugh. With the last two he collaborated in producing *Monsieur de Pourceaugnac, or Squire Trelooby*, which was performed on March 30, 1704, at Lincoln's Inn Fields. Walsh's friendship with Pope and his suggested corrections of the latter's *Pastorals* constitute his chief claim to literary remembrance.

1. The epistles and verses of Walsh in MS. Malone 9 have in some places been corrected. Whether these corrections are the result of Dryden's suggestions can only be conjectured. From the later letters it is certain that Dryden did make corrections in Walsh's poetry.

Letter 13 . . . page 26

From the *Letterbook of Sir George Etherege,* British Museum, Add. MS. 11513, f. 179. Miss Sybil Rosenfeld published the complete *Letterbook* in 1928. As this letter and the following suggest, Dryden and Etherege had been on intimate terms before the latter went as envoy to Ratisbon. They had been members of the same literary set, which included also Dorset and Sir Charles Sedley. In 1676 Dryden wrote an epilogue for Etherege's play, *The Man of Mode.*

1. The Lord Chamberlain was Dryden's patron, the Earl of Mulgrave.

2. I think that the son mentioned here is Charles, for in the letter in answer to this Etherege expresses the hope of a letter from him. Because of his modest literary pretensions, Charles probably knew Etherege before he left England for Ratisbon. Lord Middleton was one of the Secretaries of State.

3. Lord Sunderland was Robert Spencer, the second Earl, and son of Dorothy Spencer ("Sacharissa"). He became a powerful member of James's government. An enemy of Dryden's patron, Lawrence Hyde, he was able to remove him from his Treasury position a month before this letter was written. See the general note to Letter 10.

4. Wycherley had languished in Fleet Prison, and had suffered illnesses on several occasions. See Willard Connely, *Brawny Wycherley* (New York, 1930).

5. The coffeehouse was probably Will's, owned by Will Urwin, in Russell Street.

6. Cordell, or "Scum," Goodman, the actor, had played the role of Alexander in Nat Lee's *The Rival Queens,* which had been acted a few months before this letter, on October 27, 1686, at Whitehall. I have found no record of the duel mentioned here.

7. White Stick; i.e., white staff, the symbol of office, especially that of Lord Treasurer.

8. For the significance of this passage in respect to Dryden's position among the moderate Catholics, see L. I. Bredvold, *The Intellectual Milieu of John Dryden* ("University of Michigan Publications in Language and Literature," XII, Ann Arbor, 1934), p. 183. Professor Bredvold believes that the fable of the Swallows in Dryden's *Hind and the Panther* becomes an "expression of Catholic disapproval of James and his policies."

Letter 14 . . . page 28

From the *Letterbook of Sir George Etherege*, British Museum, Add. MS. 11513, f. 64v. It is in answer to Dryden's letter of February 16.

1. Dryden's diffidence and ineptness in Court circles, which the poet often alludes to, seem to have been recognized by his intimates. The reference here, of course, may apply merely to the passage in Dryden's earlier letter.

2. Sir Henry Shere was attached at Tangier, where Dryden's uncle, John Creed, was Secretary to the Tangiers Commission. In the last months of 1692 Sir Henry published *The History of Polybius*, for which Dryden wrote a Character of Polybius.

Letter 15 . . . page 30

In the Pierpont Morgan Library, New York. It is without date, and there is nothing to suggest one. It seems to be the answer to Walsh's first letter to Dryden (see above, Letter 12). It is odd to find Dryden addressing the young Walsh as "padron." I date it in 1690, only because it appears to me to initiate the correspondence between the two men, which flourished during this and the succeeding few years.

Letter 16 . . . page 31

In the British Museum, Add. MS. 10434, f. 8r-9r. It has not hitherto been printed. The date can only be guessed at—sometime in 1690; for Walsh mentions his *Dialogue Concerning Women*, which was advertised in the *London Gazette* for April 20, 1691. The letter is a copy in Walsh's hand, preserved in a small manuscript volume of letters, addresses, elegies, and verses. Apparently Walsh wrote out his correspondence in rough draft in this volume, and later transferred it to note paper for sending. The manuscript is in a good state of preservation, though a few folios are torn at the edges. An accurate transcript is made difficult by many interlinear corrections and insertions.

1. Walsh's source for this statement is, I believe, to be found in Rymer's translation of Rapin's *Réflexions sur la Poétique d'Aristote et sur les ouvrages des poëtes anciens et modernes* (1674). In Rymer's translation occurs this passage: "An Epigram is little worth, unless it be admirable; and it is so rare to make them admirable, that 'tis sufficient to have made one in a Man's life" (*Monsieur Rapin's Reflections on Aristotle's Treatise of Poesie*, London, 1694, p. 154).

2. The epigram is Martial's, XI, lxxxi:

> Cum sene communem vexat spado Dindymus aeglen
> et iacet in medio sicca puella toro.

Viribus hic, operi non est hic utilis annis:
    ergo sine effectu prurit utrique labor,
supplex illa rogat pro se miserisque duobus,
    hunc iuvenem facias, hunc, Cytherea, virum.

3. This elegy is an imitation of the *Amores*, III, xi. It is a re-crimination against the false and fickle mistress, but at the same time a recognition and appreciation of the power of her beauty. Walsh's poem is entitled "Elegy to his False Mistress," and is a close imitation of Ovid's poem. It was published in his *Letters and Poems, Amorous and Gallant* (1692), p. 85.

4. See general note above.

Letter 17 . . . page 33

I do not know the whereabouts of this letter. The present text is that of Robert Bell, who first printed it in *The Poetical Works of John Dryden* (1854), I, 68. Although Bell does not attempt to date the letter very closely, it is obviously in answer to Walsh's letter (No. 16). I should therefore date it early in 1691.

1. The reference is to Bernard le Bovier de Fontenelle's *Entretiens sur la pluralité des Mondes* (1686), which was designed to popularize Descartes' theories of astronomy.

2. Dryden refers here to Father Jean Goulu, of the Feuillant order, author of *Lettres de Phyllarque à Ariste où il est traité de l'éloquence française* (Paris, 1627). The criticism on Balzac will be found in Letter XXI. What Goulu actually wrote was "la suitte de quinze petits mots, dont les treize sont monosyllabes." In the dedication to the *Æneid* Dryden mentions the same criticism.

3. Walsh's epigram, called "Gripe and Shifter," appeared in 1692 in *Letters and Poems, Amorous and Gallant*. The text is as follows:

    Rich Gripe does all his Thoughts and Cunning bend,
    T'encrease that Wealth he wants the Soul to spend.
    Poor Shifter does his whole Contrivance set
    To spend the Wealth, he wants the Sense to get.
    How happy wou'd appear to each his Fate,
    Had Gripe his Humour, or he Gripe's Estate!
    Kind Fate and Fortune, blend 'em if you can,
    And of two Wretches, make one happy Man.

4. It will be observed that Walsh amends his lines precisely as Dryden suggests. Though it has always been known that Dryden was eager to aid younger writers with suggestions and criticism, these letters, I believe, provide the sole example of the poet's definite corrections of a particular poem for another poet.

5. Dryden reverts to—and objects to—Walsh's criticism of Martial's verse (see Letter 16).

6. This is in Walsh's *Dialogue Concerning Women*, which Dryden was now reading in manuscript.

Letter 18 . . . page 36

In the British Museum, Add. MS. 10434, f. 9v-10r. It has not hitherto been printed. It is an answer to the preceding letter and should be dated probably in 1691.

1. *All whole* was corrected in the third verse; *ease y^t pain* was corrected in the penultimate verse.

Letter 19 . . . page 38

In the British Museum, Add. MS. 10434, f. 29r-30v. It has not hitherto been printed. The date again is uncertain, but probably early in 1691.

1. That Walsh's purpose did not remain undetected is shown by a manuscript satire, now in the Folger Shakespeare Library, entitled "On the Author of a Dialogue concerning Women, pretended to be writ in Defence of the Sex." Dryden comes in for a severe attack, which I believe has hitherto escaped notice. A few excerpts suggest the anonymous writer's attitude toward Dryden, Walsh, and the *Dialogue:*

> Now to the witling Club at Will's he's [Dryden] Guide,
> As Brother Hodge was to the Levite-Tribe;
> Where he in Numbers trains admiring Fop,
> And with his Hind and Panther brings him up.
> One of these Brats, dress'd up in Shape of Satyr,
> Comes forth to be the Ladie's Vindicator;
> And, since for Chivalry he claims no Warrant,
> Instead of Knight, sets up for Poet Errant. . . .
> The beauteous Sex may set their Hearts at rest,
> Of all their Patrons sure this is the best!
> This great dead-doing Champion of the Quill
> Will all the Fry of lewd Lampooners kill! . . .
> But when the boasted Matter I had read,
> I found my Expectation was misled,
> And that the Author, tho' he does pretend
> To do them service, was no Woman's Friend. . . .
> He that but strictly marks the whole Design
> May trace the Prefacer in every Line;
> And tho' he does not own the wanton Ape,
> He nurs'd the Cub, and lick'd him into Shape.
> And, Ladies, now without the Help of Day,
> And brandishes his Pen against your Credit,
> 'Tis Mr Eat-finger himself that did it.

After more verses on Dryden he ends with these couplets:

> This is the Fool, fair Ladyes, that does haunt thee
> That will from Dressing-room to Play gallant yee;
> Wa-sh he is call'd; what name so much renown'd
> Thro all the Realms of Nonsence can be found?

2. Dryden of course wrote this preface. An examination of it shows that he followed almost literally the suggestions made here by Walsh.

3. In the *Dialogue*, contrary to what is implied here, Walsh speaks only briefly of Dryden and mentions none of his works by name.

4. Only "Written to Eugenia" appears on the title page—which would seem to have been sufficient for his purpose as outlined here.

Letter 20 . . . page 40

In the British Museum, Add. MS. 10434, f. 55v-57v. It has not hitherto been printed. It is dated by Walsh August 13, 1691.

1. I have not been able to find that Walsh ever proceeded with his elaborate plan. There is, at any rate, no record of its publication.

2. Marin Cureau de la Chambre (1594-1669), author of *Les Caractères des passions*, which was published in five volumes in 1640. It was regarded in its time as a good physiology.

3. Jean Louis Guez de Balzac (1594-1654). His *Lettres*, upon which his reputation rests, were first published in 1624. He was well known in England.

4. Vincent Voiture (1594-1648). Walsh apparently refers here to the letters of gallantry which Voiture wrote to Mlle. Paulet, Mme. Saintot, and Mme. de Soblé.

5. The War of the Grand Alliance, 1689-1697.

6. What Walsh means, I believe, is that it is no more a breach of patriotism to mention the French in a dialogue than to translate French books into English—a practice which continued throughout the war.

7. This request was answered, as is apparent from the next letter of Walsh's (Letter 21); but Dryden's answer is not extant.

8. After some difficulties, *Cleomenes* was acted in May, 1692. Southerne, in his Epistle Dedicatory to *The Wives' Excuse* (for which Dryden wrote a prefatory poem), boasts that when Dryden fell ill in the summer of 1691, "he bequeathed to my care the writing of half the last act of his tragedy of *Cleomenes*." In the *Gentleman's Journal* for February, 1691/2 (p. 27), Peter Motteux records that "Mr. Dryden has compleated a new *Tragedy*, intended shortly for the Stage. . . ." In March, he writes, "We are to have . . . Mr. Dryden's *Cleomenes* very shortly." On April 12, "it was to have appear'd upon the Stage on Saturday last . . . but Orders came from Her Majesty to hinder it being Acted, so none can tell when it shall be play'd." On May 14,

however, he records that it has been acted with great applause, and devotes a considerable space to an appreciative criticism of it. For the copyright, Dryden received thirty guineas from Tonson. The poet's receipt for that amount, now in the possession of Admiral Sir Lewis Clinton-Baker, of Bayfordbury, Herts., is dated October 6, 1691, which suggests that the play was then completed—or at least nearly enough so for Tonson to risk his money.

9. The projected work on the priesthood, if undertaken, was never completed. This remains the sole mention, so far as I know, of such a work. Dryden has again and again been castigated for his severity, both in his poems and plays, toward priests of all religions. The careful reader of Dryden, however, realizes that he does not attack priests per se, but only bad priests and the abuses of the priesthood. Although it may be idle conjecture to guess what his work on the priesthood would have been, I hazard the suggestion that it probably would have treated *good* priests and the proper province and the decorum of priesthood. In 1699 Dryden wrote a version of Chaucer's Good Parson at the request of Pepys, and included it in the *Fables*.

10. This probably refers to the marriage of Jane, daughter of Sir William Leveson-Gower (of Trentham, Staffordshire) to Henry, Lord Hyde. In his Dedication of *Amphitryon*, which appeared in October, 1690, to Leveson-Gower, Dryden mentions her, and calls her Berenice. In the later dedication of *Cleomenes* to Lawrence Hyde, Earl of Rochester, he records that he had read the play to a group of ladies, among whom was Berenice. To Hyde, and Lady Hyde incidentally, Dryden gives credit for intercession with the Queen to allow the presentation of *Cleomenes*. Dryden's relationship with Leveson-Gower is rather vague; but in the Dedication to *Amphitryon* he recalls with pleasure having been entertained at Trentham.

11. Abberley is a village in Worcestershire, about fifteen miles north-west of Worcester.

Letter 21 . . . page 44

In the British Museum, Add. MS. 10434, f. 59v-61r. It has not hitherto been printed. The date is probably September or October, 1691. The reference in the first sentence obviously is to Dryden's illness of the late summer. This letter is in answer to Dryden's reply, not extant, to Walsh's letter (Letter 19).

1. I once thought that this referred to Jane Leveson-Gower; but since she had married Lawrence Hyde, Earl of Rochester, the reference is not to her. I am at a loss to suggest the identity of the person mentioned.

2. Walsh probably refers to Book III of the *Book of the Courtier*, and Book IV, secs. 49-67.

3. Alvarotti degli Speroni (1500-1588). His *Dialoghi* came out in Venice in 1542, and was translated into French in 1551. He was regarded in his own time as an authoritative voice on literary matters.

4. Alessandro Tassoni (1565-1635). The work referred to is probably *Varietà di pensieri* (Modena, 1612).

5. Mario Equicola (1460-1541), historian and philosopher. His *Della Natura d'Amore* was published in 1525 and translated into French in 1554. Divided into six books, it treats methodically the questions of the philosophy of love.

6. For La Chambre, see Letter 20, note 2.

7. Plato's dialogue on love is the *Symposium;* the one on beauty is probably the *Hippias Major,* now usually considered spurious.

8. One can only guess that Dryden's reply to Walsh's enthusiastic proposal was not too encouraging.

9. Demetrius Phalereus, a pupil of Theophrastus, was distinguished as orator and statesman. He governed Athens from 317-307 B.C. The essay on rhetoric, which was formerly attributed to him, and which Walsh here refers to, is now dated about the first century A.D., and attributed to another Demetrius. The reference here is to par. 224f. of *On Style.*

10. *Lettres familières à M. Chapelain* (Amsterdam, 1651); *Lettres de M. de Balzac à M. de Conrart* (Paris, 1658).

11. Lipsius was the Latinized name of Joest Lips (1547-1606), the great Belgian scholar.

12. Boileau's imitation of Balzac's style may be found in a letter to the Duc de Vivonne (Gidel, *Œuvres complètes de Boileau,* Paris, 1878, pp. 134-141). Inserted in this letter are two letters in their own styles from Balzac and Voiture, in the Elysian Fields. Walsh is quoting directly from both.

13. By "Character" Walsh apparently means "style," using it in the technical sense it had in Greek rhetoric. Such a use is found occasionally in the period.

Letter 22 . . . page 48

In the possession of the present Lord Sackville at Knole. Part of it was printed by V. Sackville-West in *Knole and the Sackvilles* (London, 1922), p. 149. More recently the letter was printed by Charles J. Phillips in the *History of the Sackville Family,* I, 444. It is addressed to Charles, Earl of Dorset, and dated "Octob: 7th Thursday." Since the rumor of the Queen Dowager's departure for Portugal, which finally took place in March, 1692, was now current, the year of the letter must be 1691. October 7 in this year fell on a Wednesday; Dryden may possibly have made a mistake in the day of the week. Furthermore, he here mentions his illness alluded to in Letter 21, which I have dated in September or October, 1691.

1. I have been unable to identify Mr. Munson.

2. Louis Duras, Lord Chamberlain to the Queen Dowager, to whom was intrusted the care of Somerset House, when the Queen left for Portugal in March, 1692 *(D. N. B.).*

3. The Earl of Dorset, who remained one of Dryden's best friends and patrons to the end of his life, at this time held the post of Lord Chamberlain. A few months after this letter was written, Dryden addressed to him *A Discourse Concerning the Original and Progress of Satire,* which was published, as a dedication to the *Satires* of Juvenal, toward the end of the following October (see advertisement in the *London Gazette,* No. 2813, Oct. 24-27, 1692). In this address Dryden makes handsome acknowledgment of the favors received from Dorset. See Brice Harris, *Charles Sackville, Sixth Earl of Dorset* ("Illinois Studies in Language and Literature," XXVI, Nos. 3-4, Urbana, Illinois, 1940).

Letter 23 . . . page 49

The whereabouts of this letter I do not know. Through the kindness of Mr. James M. Osborn I am able to incorporate Malone's corrections for his projected second edition. Since the letters from Dryden, mentioned here by Tonson, were dated October 3 and 10, I should assume that the bookseller's reply was made not more than a month later. I suggest November, 1692, as a better date, therefore, than January or February, 1693, which Malone advanced.

1. The Third Miscellany, or *Examen Poeticum,* came out in July, 1693.

2. Through the influence of the Earl of Dorset, the then Lord Chamberlain, Nahum Tate, was appointed Poet Laureate on December 24, 1692, in place of Thomas Shadwell, who had died on November 19 or 20. Tate's "undertaking" was apparently *The Metamorphoses.* It was not published, however, until 1697; it was called *Ovids Metamorphosis,* and described as translated by several hands. Tate probably served as general editor, for he signed the preface addressed to the Earl of Portland.

3. Hero and Leander were left out; but the Last Parting of Hector and Andromache from the sixth book of the *Iliad* was included, as well as the whole of Book I of the *Metamorphoses,* the Fable of Iphis and

Ianthe from the ninth, and the Fable of Acis, Polyphemus, and Galatea, from the thirteenth, along with numerous shorter pieces.

4. Peter Motteux, publisher of the *Gentleman's Journal*, had been giving Dryden much favorable critical attention. See Letter 20, note 7.

5. Tonson's penny-pinching seems a bit fantastic at this distance; but to Dryden—in 1692—the procuring of a few extra pounds was a matter of great import. This lack of a definite agreement with Tonson perhaps strengthened Dryden's resolve to obtain a legal agreement for the *Virgil*, less than two years later. See my articles, "Some Notes on Dryden," *Review of English Studies*, XIII (1937), 297-306, and "The Publication and Profits of Dryden's *Virgil*," *Publications of the Modern Language Association*, LIII (1938), 807-812.

6. Dryden's translations from Juvenal and Persius were published hardly a month before this letter was written. The project, however, had been under way for some time, and was nearly ready for the press in February, 1692. It was held up to allow Dryden time to complete his translation of Persius. The dedication to Dorset was dated as early as August 18, but the volume was advertised only at the end of October, in the *London Gazette*, October 24-27. Dryden's share of Juvenal consisted of 2,280 lines from the first, third, sixth, tenth, and sixteenth satires. I do not know whether he received fifty guineas for it.

Letter 24 . . . page 52

In the Pierpont Morgan Library. It was first printed by Bell. The letter is dated by Dryden, "May 9th or 10th." Since he had completed half of *Love Triumphant*, which was acted in December, 1693, the year must be 1693. In this year Tuesday fell on May 9.

1. Apparently Dryden decided to "let him go"; for an examination of the records of Chancery and the Common Pleas has failed to reveal the poet in a lawsuit.

2. D'Urfey's farce was *The Richmond Heiress*. Doggett (Solon) played the part of Quickwit, and Mrs. Bracegirdle that of Fulvia. See Robert S. Forsythe, *A Study of the Plays of Thomas D'Urfey* ("Western Reserve Studies," I, Nos. 2-3, Cleveland, 1916), pp. 91 ff.

3. This was probably Reading, a singer at Drury Lane. In 1695 he and Pate (another singer) were discharged and fined for engaging in a riot at Dog Tavern, Drury Lane. They were soon reinstated (Grove, *Dictionary of Music and Musicians*, III, 80).

4. She was an actress and singer in Betterton's company, and was one of those who refused to sign Betterton's petition to the Lord Chamberlain in 1694 (Allardyce Nicoll, *A History of Restoration Drama*, p. 341).

5. The Duke of Richmond was the son of Charles II by Louise Quérouaille, Duchess of Portsmouth. He was born on July 29, 1672, and given the name Charles Lennox. He was created Duke of Richmond in 1675.

6. The Duke of St. Albans was born on May 8, 1670, the son of Nell Gwynn and the King. He was given the name of Beauclerk; and in 1684 was created the Duke of St. Albans.

7. Dryden's information on the course of the war came apparently from the newssheets of the day, which were full of speculation and of interpretation of the moves on the Continent.

8. Walsh was trying to obtain a position in the Exchequer. See Letter 25, note 1.

9. This preface, which may have been suggested by Walsh as a return favor for Dryden's preface to his *Dialogue Concerning Women*, seems not to have been written. It doubtless would have been a learned treatise urging the claims of the modern drama. As such it would have taken its place in the developing quarrel of the ancients and moderns. It should be recalled that Rymer's *Short View of Tragedy*, extremely critical of Dryden, had appeared in the closing weeks of 1692. And Dryden seems here to be reserving for himself an attack on Rymer. See Letters 26 and 28.

10. Thomas Doggett, who had played the part of Solon in D'Urfey's *The Marriage Hater Match'd* in 1691. This passage suggests the care that Dryden exercised in preparing a play for the stage. The play was *Love Triumphant*, his last.

11. Dryden seems to have been especially fond of these two young dramatists. He thought so highly of Southerne that he allowed him to write half of the last act of *Cleomenes* (1692), and he prefixed verses of commendation to Southerne's *The Wives' Excuse* in 1692. Congreve remained his close friend to the end of his life. Though Dryden did not hail the appearance of Congreve's first play, *The Old Bachelor*, he wrote verses to Congreve upon the publication of his second, *The Double Dealer*, in 1694. In the same year Congreve was Dryden's witness to the agreement with Tonson for the *Virgil*.

12. Wycherley's poems did not appear until many years later—in 1704. Though they were ready at this time, proposals for subscriptions were not published until November, 1696. In January, 1700, Wycherley brought suit against Briscoe, his publisher, for failure to publish and to account for subscription money. See Howard P. Vincent, "William Wycherley's *Miscellany Poems*," *Philological Quarterly*, XVI (1937), 145-148.

13. Dryden's sons may have gone to Rome only recently. A letter from Cardinal Howard, dated at Rome on June 30, 1693, gives an in-

teresting side light on the poet and his family at this time. The Cardinal, a distant relation of Lady Elizabeth Dryden, was looking after the
affairs of James II at the Vatican. "Now that we are in expectation of
his Majesty's speedy restoration, so many will petition for favours, that
I must also be one of them beforehand, begging of his Majesty . . .
that here being two brothers, Catholic gentlemen, called Charles and
John Draytons, sons to the famous poet laureat Drayton in London;
one whereof I have, in the interim, got a place of *cameriera di honora*,
with our old man; and the other liveth with me. But they always de-
siring to serve their natural King, and both their father and they having
been always faithful, would have gone to serve him in France, had it
not been to put him to straits, among so many others, for their main-
tenance. Wherefore, my humble request is, that his Majesty will please
to make them his gentlemen ushers daily waiters in ordinary in his
presence-chamber, or grooms of his privy-chamber, at his return into
England; which honour I am confident they will both as faithfully as
decently perform; their father being a convert, and their mother a
catholic sister to the lord Berkshire" (James Macpherson, *Original
Papers*, London, 1775, I, 470).

14. At Worcester on April 30, some merchants arrived to buy corn
for export. The rabble seized what they had bought, upon which the
mayor dispersed the rioters and put the ringleaders in jail. On May 1
the rioters again got together, succeeded in delivering their leaders
from jail, and marched four miles to break into storage houses and divide the corn. This was the state of affairs when Dryden wrote the letter. Later, in June, four of the rioters were sentenced to death. See
The Life and Times of Anthony Wood, ed. Andrew Clark (Oxford,
1892-1900), III, 422, 425.

Letter 25. . . page 56

In the Pierpont Morgan Library. It was first printed by Bell. It
can be dated August 17, 1693, for the fleet anchored in Torbay on
Wednesday, August 16 (*Cal. State Papers, Domestic, 1693*, p. 270).

1. The position which Walsh was attempting to get was that of
Teller of the Exchequer. Henry Carey—as Dryden reports here—was
sworn into that position on July 17, after presenting a security bond of
£3,000 of his own, and £500 each of eight other persons. See *Cal.
Treasury Books*, X, pt. 1, pp. 276, 285.

2. That is, the coach to Northamptonshire, where he went the following week.

3. The book of Miscellanies published by Tonson was *Examen Poeticum*. In Motteux's *Gentleman's Journal* for June it was announced

for future publication, and Tonson invited the "ingenious" to contribute what might be proper. The response seems to have been immediate; for in July Motteux announced, prematurely as it would appear, that *Examen Poeticum* had been published. Besides translations from Ovid's *Metamorphoses*, Dryden contributed some minor pieces, and reprints of his earlier work, notably the *Ode to Mrs. Anne Killigrew*.

4. Herringman's *Miscellanies* was probably that published by F. Saunders (who was Herringman's man) and advertised in the Term Catalogues for Easter, 1694, as *A Collection of Poems on Several Occasions written by the Right Honourable The Earls of Mulgrave, Rochester, Roscommon and Orrery*, etc. Dryden's name is also included in the list of authors.

5. Admiral Sir George Rooke and his action with the Smyrna fleet I discuss in the notes to Letter 28. Dryden's information on the events of the war seems to have been fairly accurate; it was doubtless gathered at the coffeehouse and from the numerous newsletters and papers. De Tourville was the French Commander of the Fleet at Brest, which took part in the defeat of Rooke, about June 6. Huy was reported taken by the French on July 18. The Duke de Lorges was Marshal of France, commanding the troops against William. The news of the movement of the armies on the Continent reached England toward late July or early August. See the *Historical and Political Monthly Mercury* for July and August, 1693.

Letter 26 . . . page 58

In the Pierpont Morgan Library. It was first printed by Malone. The date is August 30 [1693]. The year is determined by the fact that the *Third Miscellany* was published in August, 1693.

1. Apparently Dryden was visiting at the Manor of Clapton, which was held by Sir Matthew Dudley, who had inherited the estate and baronetcy from his father, Sir William Dudley. Clapton was only a short distance east of Tichmarsh. Sir Matthew was later (1701) a Deputy Lieutenant for Northamptonshire (*Cal. State Papers, Domestic, 1700-1702*, p. 257), and still later a Commissioner of the Customs. He became a friend of Swift, and is often mentioned in the *Journal to Stella*.

2. The *Third Miscellany, or Examen Poeticum*, was dedicated to Lord Radclyffe, who succeeded to the title of Earl of Derwentwater in 1696. Dryden doubtless expected for the dedication an honorarium, which was not forthcoming.

3. Dryden had said: "No government has ever been, or ever can be, wherein timeservers and blockheads will not be uppermost. The per-

sons are only chang'd, but the same jugglings in state, the same hypocrisy in religion, the same self-interest and mismanagement, will remain for ever. Blood and money will be lavish'd in all ages, only for the preferment of new faces, with old sciences."

4. *A Short View of Tragedy*, which appeared in December, 1692. He lashed Rymer and his fellows in the Dedication to Radclyffe.

Letter 27 . . . page 60

In the William Andrews Clark Memorial Library. It is dated Wednesday "the 13th of 7ber." Malone, who first printed it, assigns it to 1695, but it should be dated 1693; for obviously it is written from the same place (and a fortnight later) as Letter 26; and September 13 was a Wednesday in 1693. Mr. Dudley was doubtless William Dudley, brother of Sir Matthew Dudley, whom I have identified in Letter 26. In that letter to Tonson, dated August 30, Dryden says that he intends to come up to town at least a week before Michaelmas. In this letter he has taken a place in the coach which will bring him to town just about a week before Michaelmas.

Letter 28 . . . page 61

In the Pierpont Morgan Library. It was first printed by Bell. It is dated December 12 [1693]. The letter from Walsh, which Dryden refers to, is lost; it doubtless outlined the projected preface to Dryden's play. See Letter 24, note 9.

1. Dryden had already discoursed on this, drawing the same example from Mascardi, in his *Discourse Concerning the Original and Progress of Satire*, which was dated August 18, 1692.

2. The play, *Love Triumphant*, was acted probably in January. Evelyn records that on January 11, 1693/4, he supped at Edward Sheldon's, where Dryden read the prologue and epilogue of his "valedictory play, now shortly to be acted."

3. Walsh, so far as I can discover, published no book of criticism in 1693 or 1694.

4. *The Double Dealer*. As the superscription to the letter makes evident, Dryden sent the play to Walsh. It had probably just come from the press, for it was advertised in the *London Gazette* for December 4-7, 1693. It had been acted in November or in late October.

5. In May, 1693, Admiral Sir George Rooke was appointed to convoy some four hundred merchant ships, known popularly as the Smyrna fleet, on the outbound Mediterranean trade. With him were the joint Admirals, Henry Killigrew and Sir Clowdisley Shovell. Assuming incorrectly that the French fleet under De Tourville was at

Brest, the joint Admirals left Rooke to convoy the merchant ships alone. The French attacked and defeated him. With the remnants of his fleet Rooke sailed for Madeira, and from there to Ireland.

6. Edward Russell, Admiral of the Fleet. In spite of a naval victory over the French in May, 1692, he was dismissed from his command; but in November, 1693, he was reinstated, and in May, 1694, appointed first Lord of the Admiralty. It is to this appointment that Dryden refers.

7. Thomas Osborne, Earl of Danby, to whom Dryden had dedicated *All for Love*. The Triennial Bill provided that the Parliament then sitting should cease to exist on January 1, 1694, and that no future Parliament should last longer than three years. Dryden was correct in his prediction: it was thrown out in the Commons.

8. Robert Squib, who was called to the House of Commons on December 9 to make an accounting of the money paid for secret service and to Members of Parliament by William Jephson, deceased, whose accounts Squib had in his posssession. See *Journal of the House of Commons*, XI (1693-97), 26, 28.

9. DuBart was a notorious French privateer. Narcissus Luttrell records, on December 9, that DuBart had seized two convoys, the *Warrington* and the *Milford* (*Brief Relation*, III, 237).

10. The formal—and legal—agreement with Tonson was dated June 15, 1694.

11. This essay was published in the so-called *Fourth Miscellany*, early in 1694, and reprinted with only a few changes in the *Virgil* three years later.

12. Apparently these were the verses to be published before Wycherley's poems, which were destined not to appear until 1704.

Letter 29 . . . page 65

First printed in *Letters upon Several Occasions* (London, 1696), p. 46. It is there dated "Jan. 1693/4."

1. Dennis's words suggest that this letter is the first he had ever written to Dryden.

2. The reference to "your preparatives" is undoubtedly to the projected translation of Vergil, already mentioned in Dryden's letter to Walsh. It seems likely that the "town" generally was aware of Dryden's preparations for the work.

Letter 30 . . . page 67

First printed in *Letters upon Several Occasions* (London, 1696), pp. 49 ff. It is there dated "March 3, 1693/4."

1. Probably this letter is an answer to Dennis's first (Letter 29).

2. I believe this is an oblique reference to his *The Impartial Critic* and the *Miscellanies in Verse and Prose,* both of which appeared in the preceding year.

Letter 31 . . . page 70

Malone's conjecture as to date—March 1693/4—is doubtless close to the mark, for this letter seems to be an answer to Dennis's of March 3 (Letter 30). The text is from *Letters upon Several Occasions* (London, 1696), pp. 53 ff., where it was first printed.

1. Dryden here refers to Charles Perrault's *Parallèle des anciens et des modernes* (1688), which lauded modern progress in science and art, and which was a part of the long controversy over the respective merits of the ancients and the moderns.

2. Dennis had published very little before the time of this letter: *Miscellanies in Verse and Prose* came out in 1693. *Poems in Burlesque* had been printed in 1692. What perhaps drew Dryden's eulogy of Dennis as a critic was the latter's *The Impartial Critick, or, Some Observations upon a late book entitled a Short View of Tragedy, written by Mr. Rymer,* which appeared in 1693. At nearly the same time Dryden, in *Examen Poeticum,* was letting loose a blast at Rymer. For Dennis, see H. G. Paul, *John Dennis: His Life and Criticism* (New York, 1911), and Edward N. Hooker, *The Critical Works of John Dennis* (Baltimore, 1939).

3. In Canto III of *L'art poétique.*

4. In the *Discourse Concerning the Original and Progress of Satire* Dryden had written: "Christian poets have not been acquainted with their own strength. If they had search'd the Old Testament as they ought, they might there have found the machines which are proper for their work. . . . The perusing of one chapter in the Prophecy of Daniel, and accommodating what there they find with the principles of Platonic philosophy as it is now Christianiz'd, would have made the ministry of angels as strong an engine for the working up of heroic poetry . . . as that of the ancients has been to raise theirs by all the fables of their gods. . . ." On this passage W. P. Ker remarks: "Dryden was thinking of the Platonic opinion about daemons as intermediary between heaven and earth. The idea of tutelar angels was familiar with the Platonists of Dryden's time" (*Essays of John Dryden,* II, 280).

5. As Dryden had reason to know: in number and in virulence the attacks on him probably surpass those on any other figure of the time.

6. The friend mentioned here is almost impossible to identify. It may have been Walsh, who was also a great friend of Wycherley. If it was Walsh, the letter of Wycherley's, which Dryden read and approved, must have served as an effective deterrent to his amorous inclination; for Walsh remained unmarried.

7. From the *Æneid*, VI, 608-609. Dryden translated the lines:

> Caenus, a woman once, and once a man,
> By ending in the sex she first began.

8. Wycherley's marriage to the Countess of Drogheda proved most unhappy for him: the Countess was inordinately jealous and domineering (see Willard Connely, *Brawny Wycherley*, New York, 1930).

Letter 32 . . . page 74

In the William Andrews Clark Memorial Library. Malone, who first printed it, places it April, 1695, which is probably close.

1. Apparently Dryden freely passed his manuscripts about among his friends. This practice with respect to the *Virgil* must have served to generate a great deal of interest in the translation among the "town."

2. The £50 mentioned here are difficult to explain. They may have constituted payment for Æneids 1-4, given by Tonson to Sheldon, and in turn given to Dryden. Yet at the end of the letter, Dryden speaks of when and where he may receive the £50. The first mention of the amount, of course, could refer to an entirely different transaction; i.e., Dryden's payment of a personal debt to Sheldon, which forced him to overwork himself in order to collect £50 from Tonson upon the completion of Æneid 4.

3. Malone's explanation of this sentence (I, i, 38) is not very satisfactory. What Dryden means, I believe, is this: if the second subscription prove popular, and if it be fully subscribed, then he will take so much the more care because of the additional profit. According to his agreement with Tonson, the proposal for second subscribers (at two guineas) was to be made after the sixth Æneid had been completed; that is, four months or more after the date of the present letter —perhaps between August and October, 1695. The proposal for second subscribers, written in Dryden's hand and signed by him, is included in notes to Letter 34. See also "Some Notes on Dryden," *Review of English Studies*, XIII (1937), 297-306, in which I dated that document between April and June, 1696.

4. The coinage at this time was in a deplorable state and becoming worse. Because of the clipping and adulteration that had been going on

for some years, silver currency was greatly depreciated: "Five pounds in cash was scarcely worth 40s, with the result that the guinea, nominally equivalent to 20s rose to 30s in value." Coins of brass, iron, and copper, silvered over, were freely circulated. See W. M. Acres, *The Bank of England from Within* (Oxford, 1931), I, 66.

5. The guineas referred to here are Dryden's share in the first subscribers' initial payment of three guineas. The £50 were in all probability payment for Æneids 1-4. See note 2 above.

6. Richard Maitland, Earl of Lauderdale. The "decorations" were his coat of arms to be printed in the *Virgil*. In the Dedication of the *Æneid* Dryden records that "the late Earl of Lauderdail sent me over [from France] his new translation of the Æneis, which he had ended before I engaged in the same design." Lauderdale's translation, which Dryden used, was not published until 1718. The Earl died in exile in Paris in 1695.

Letter 33 . . . page 76

In the Pierpont Morgan Library. It was first printed by Malone. It is dated merely June 8, but 1695 is the only year possible. The poet had probably just finished the fifth Æneid.

1. According to his agreement with Tonson, the second subscription edition was to have been launched after the sixth Æneid was complete. Therefore it seems probable that the halfway mark had now been reached, and that the meeting arranged for in this letter was for the purpose not only of settling financial details but also of wording proposals for the second subscriptions. See notes to the following letter.

2. This was perhaps Walter Aston, of the Aston family of Cheshire. He succeeded to the title of Lord Aston of Forfar in 1714. What his offices were in respect to the agreement for the *Virgil* I am not sure; but it appears from Dryden's words that he was in part responsible for the making of the agreement. Though difficult to make out, the signature appended to the legal agreement as Tonson's witness is, I believe, his.

3. See "The Publication and Profits of Dryden's *Virgil*," cited above, for a detailed discussion of these accounts.

4. And probably as a witness for Dryden, since he had served Dryden in that capacity at the time of the original agreement.

Letter 34 . . . page 77

In the William Andrews Clark Memorial Library. It was first printed by Malone. Dryden has dated it October 29. The year must be 1695. During the sixteen months since the agreement was signed,

Dryden had completed seven books of the *Æneid*, and the *Pastorals* and the *Georgics*.

1. That is, the third payment of £50.

2. The "thirty shillings upon every book" is difficult to explain. Dryden's share of the first subscriptions was two guineas; for the second there seems to have been no definite agreement. It may be that he was to receive thirty shillings of the two guineas charged the second subscribers; yet that hardly seems an agreement which Tonson would make. Perhaps the thirty shillings is in reality only a guinea, for the value of money, as we have seen, was constantly shifting. I assume, therefore, that the "thirty shillings" would be the one guinea on each of the second subscriptions.

3. The manuscript advertisement for the second subscriptions—now in Cambridge University Library, Add. MS. 4429(10)—is as follows:

I have intrusted my much Honourd Friend Mr. Atterbury, to receive the Money subscibed [*sic*] to me for the Translation of Virgil; & to give receipts to the Subscribers for the same.

The Price of the Book is two Guinneys: one of which is to be payd Mr. Atterbury at the time of Subscription: the other to my Stationer Mr. Tonson, at the receipt of the Book.

The Paper, print & figures of the Book, to be the best: and equall in all respects to those Books, for which five Guinneys are subscribd: only the Coats of Armes are not inserted to these Second Subscribers.

The Names and Titles of these Second Subscribers, shall be printed in a List before the Book.

By agreement betwixt me and my Stationer, no more Books are to be printed on the finest paper, than onely those, which are bespoken by the Subscribers.

All the Eclogues, all the Georgigs [*sic*], & the first six Eneids are already Translated: and I Judg the Whole Work will be finished by Lady Day next.

John Dryden

Francis Atterbury was then to be the chief gatherer, though from this letter it appears that there were many others. Kneller is of course the painter. Mr. Closterman was a portrait painter who lived in England from 1681-1713. Each of these men painted a portrait of Dryden, and it was upon their request, among others', that Dryden wrote the *Parallel of Painting and Poetry*, published in this year.

4. William Stanley, ninth Earl of Derby. The engraving to the third book of the *Æneid* was inscribed to him.

5. The Duke of Devonshire was not a subscriber.

6. Will Plowden was probably the William Plowden admitted to a fellowship at Magdalen College, along with John Dryden, Jr., in January, 1687/8, at the command of James II. Later he followed

James to France, but was eventually allowed to return to England through the influence of the Duke of Shrewsbury. See *Magdalen College and James II*, ed. J. R. Bloxam (Oxford, 1886), pp. 225, 231, 232; and George Baker, *The History and Antiquities of the County of Northampton* (London, 1822-41), I, 470.

The Countess of Macclesfield was Anne, the wife of Charles Gerard, second Earl of Macclesfield, whom she married on June 18, 1683, when she was fifteen years of age. They separated in March, 1684/5, and never thereafter lived together. She was finally divorced by her husband by Act of Parliament on April 2, 1698, and her two children by Richard (Savage), Earl Rivers, were declared illegitimate. Though the Richard Savage who was acquainted with Pope, and whom Johnson immortalized in one of his best *Lives*, claimed to be the child of this couple, he was probably an impostor.

In spite of Dryden's solicitude, the Countess was not a subscriber to the *Virgil*.

7. Philip Stanhope, second Earl of Chesterfield (1633-1713), grandfather of the more famous Earl. He held minor offices under Charles and James, but was never an important political figure.

8. Probably Thomas, the sixth Lord Petre, father of that Lord Petre who snipped Miss Fermor's curl and was therefor immortalized by Pope.

Letter 35 . . . page 79

In the William Andrews Clark Memorial Library. It is dated merely "Friday night." Malone, who first printed it, conjectured that its date was December, 1695. It seems more reasonable to date it in November, as I have done, since in the previous letter of October 29, Dryden had already completed the seventh Æneid. It would have been in Tonson's hands and circulating among Dryden's friends before December.

1. The proposals for the second subscriptions. Whether the manuscript advertisement, as printed above, represents the joint efforts of Congreve and Tonson I do not know. I rather think, however, that this was Dryden's work, and that their proposals, if actually framed, were not used. I have been unable to find a trace of them. For the acting of the play by John Dryden, Jr., I have found no precise date. Nicoll gives "1695." It may have appeared soon after this letter—in November or December. The first sentence of the letter suggests that Dryden may have been actively concerned in the staging of his son's play.

Letter 36 . . . page 80

In the William Andrews Clark Memorial Library. It was first printed by Malone. It is dated by Dryden merely "Friday, forenoon." Since the eighth Æneid is now completed (he had begun it at the end of October), I should be inclined to date the letter in late December or in early January, 1695.

1. Richard Bentley, bookseller and printer, whose establishment was in Russell Street. He and Tonson occasionally joined in issuing books. Why he was cursing the *Virgil* I do not know, unless Tonson had refused to allow him to share in publication of it. For a time Bentley was in partnership with J. Magnes, with whom he joined in publishing Dryden's *Religio Laici* in 1682. After 1688 Bentley continued in business alone, chiefly as a publisher of romances.

2. According to Malone Mr. Knight was Robert Knight, a goldsmith, who later became Cashier of the South Seas Company.

3. The money referred to here, I think, is the third payment of £50, for the fifth, sixth, seventh and eighth Æneids.

4. The first subscribers seem to have been solicited personally by Dryden, Tonson, and a number of their friends. It is difficult to know who the solicitors were, but from references scattered throughout the letters it appears that Congreve, Atterbury, Plowden, Aston, Kneller, Closterman, Ned Sheldon, and others were doing what they could to complete the list of 101. But Dryden's complaint suggests that the personal solicitation was not entirely satisfactory.

5. "The first half of Virgil" was the *Eclogues* and the *Georgics* and Books I-IV of the *Æneid*. "The other four books" were the fifth, sixth, seventh, and eighth Æneids.

6. There was: Dryden dedicated the *Georgics* to him. See the exchange of letters, *post*, between Chesterfield and Dryden.

Letter 37 . . . page 82

In the Pierpont Morgan Library. The date May 26 is given by Dryden. Malone, who first printed it, added 1696, which is right.

1. *The Husband his Own Cuckold* was published by Tonson; it carried a Dedication to Sir Robert Howard, dated at Rome, August 20, 1695.

2. See Letter 36, note 2.

Letter 38 . . . page 82

In the possession of Admiral Sir Lewis Clinton-Baker, Bayfordbury, Herts., who kindly allowed me a photostat. It was first printed by

Malone. I should date it in June. Dryden records that ten Æneids are finished. A letter in the *Historical Manuscripts Commission Reports, Hastings,* II, 280, dated September 3, reveals that "Dryden is upon the 12th book of his Virgil, the 11th is said by good judges to out do the original." If the eleventh book was being circulated in manuscript before September 3, obviously this letter in which only ten books are finished would date early in the summer; for Dryden was also burdened with writing notes to the books already translated.

1. Thomas Tompion (1639-1713), a celebrated watchmaker of the time. He is known as the father of English watchmaking.

2. Dryden's affection for his sons may be partly seen in the fact that his gift was to cost almost as much as he would receive from two books of the *Æneid*—four months' work.

Letter 39 . . . page 83

In the possession of Admiral Sir Lewis Clinton-Baker, Bayfordbury, Herts. It was first printed by Malone. There is no internal evidence which will help to fix the year. But since November 25 was a Wednesday in 1696, it seems reasonable to place it in this year.

1. Towcester.

2. His tenant's name was Harriot. It would be interesting to know what income Dryden actually had from his land, which consisted of one hundred eighty-six acres near Blakesly, Northamptonshire. The "remainder" of the rent—£16 10s.—may have represented payment for half a quarter. The annual rent would have been, at that rate, £132. In 1799 the then Lady Dryden wrote that a grandson of Dryden's tenant still rented the land, and that the rent had been increased to £182 16s. a year (see Osborn, *op. cit.,* p. 239).

Letter 40 . . . page 84

In the Pierpont Morgan Library. It was first printed by Malone. Since the last Æneid, which had been begun probably in September, 1696, was now completed, I should say that November would be near the probable date.

1. The fourth Eclogue, or Pollio, and the ninth, or Lycidas and Moeris, were printed in *Miscellany Poems* (1684). He corrected them, as he says, for reprinting in 1697. Noyes, *Dryden's Poetical Works,* Cambridge Edition, pp. 998-999, records the changes made. The ninth Eclogue was not ascribed to Dryden in the 1684 Miscellany. The phrase "in my wife's printed Miscellany" is curious. He may mean that he has made the corrections in his wife's copy of the printed text, and has sent it along for the use of the printer.

Letter 41 . . . page 85

In the British Museum, Add. MS. 19253, f. 179b. It is a copy, preserved in the letter book of the second Earl of Chesterfield, which was first printed in 1829.

1. In Letter 36, which I have dated December, 1695, written to Tonson, Dryden records a visit of Chesterfield to him, but adds, "I durst say nothing of Virgil to him, for feare there shou'd be no void place for him." Perhaps Chesterfield's friendliness on the occasion of the visit suggested him as a patron. Perhaps it should also be mentioned that gossip insists upon an affair between Chesterfield and Lady Elizabeth Dryden, before her marriage to the poet.

2. The return of James II was continually looked forward to by the Jacobites.

3. Sir Thomas Clifford, to whom, in 1673, Dryden dedicated *Amboyna*. Though Dryden's relation to Clifford has never been thoroughly worked out, it seems probable to me that Clifford, who perhaps met Dryden through Sir Robert Howard, had not a little influence on Dryden's appointment as Poet Laureate in 1668.

4. John Sheffield, Earl of Mulgrave, who had been created Marquess of Normanby in 1694.

Letter 42 . . . page 87

In the British Museum, Add. MS. 19253, f. 180a. It is a copy in the Chesterfield letter book. It was printed in 1829.

1. He possibly means that Dryden must be weary of attempting to get aid from William's government.

Letter 43 . . . page 88

In the William Andrews Clark Memorial Library. It was first printed by Malone.

1. Mr. Pate, a woolen draper with some pretensions to learning, was apparently one of the collectors for the second subscriptions to the *Virgil*. In later years Pate was friendly with Swift, who mentions him as a dinner companion. See the *Journal to Stella*, under the dates September 17, 24, and October 6, 1710.

2. Sam Atkins was perhaps Samuel Pepys's clerk. He was a subscriber to the two-guinea edition, and apparently a solicitor for it.

Letter 44 . . . page 89

In the British Museum, Add. MS. 19253, f. 181a. It is a copy from the letter book and was printed in 1829.

1. Resentments, *appreciations* (O. E. D.).

2. What this gift was, which Dryden acknowledges in the following letter, we have no way of knowing. Since the poet speaks of the "largeness" of it, it was probably a considerable gift of money.

Letter 45 . . . page 90

In the British Museum, Add. MS. 19253, f. 181b. It is a copy from the letter book. It was printed in 1829.

1. Probably a reference to L. Cornelius Sulla, the dictator.

Letter 46 . . . page 91

This letter is in the possession of the Marquess of Downshire, who kindly allowed me a copy. A portion of it has hitherto been printed, in the report of the *Historical Manuscripts Commission, Trumbull Papers*, pt. 2, p. 761. Sir William Trumbull was a Secretary of State and a Privy Councillor from May 3, 1695 to December 1, 1697. Dryden gives him credit for "recommending" the last Æneid.

1. These best friends may possibly have been priests. I do not know what his illness was at this time.

2. This was Thomas Metcalf, the bookseller. Most of the circumstances described in this letter can be followed in the *Cal. State Papers, Domestic, 1697*, pp. 300, 301, 318. On August 12 is recorded: "The Warden of the Stationer's Company and Stephens, the messenger of the press, called in. He gave an account of seizing a popish book called the *Constitutions of Innocent*, on the 11th. It is designed for the use of the English clergy, and printed in Bloomsbury for one Metcalfe, a bookseller in Drury Lane. Ordered that Metcalfe be taken up by the Duke of Shrewsbury warrant, and that the Council be acquainted with the fault." On the same day is recorded a somewhat different account (p. 301): "Warrent to Robert Stevens, messenger in ordinary, to apprehend Thomas Metcalf, bookseller, who has caused several popish and seditious books and pamphlets to be printed, particularly a book entitled *Constitutiones Clericorum Saecularium in communi viventium*, &. He is to be brought to the Duke of Shrewsbury for examination." On the day after Dryden made this plea to Sir William Trumbull, the case came up for hearing. Whether Dryden's intercession was efficacious I do not know; but presumably the case was dismissed. A brief record of the hearing is to be found on page 318: "Metcalf, the bookseller who printed *Con-*

stitutiones Innocentis, was called in. He said he had the copy from one Gerald, who used to come to his shop, but did not know what he was or where he lived. He bespoke 100 to be printed for private use."

Letter 47 . . . page 92

In the Lambeth Palace Library, Vol. 933, item 56. The manuscript is badly mutilated. I have supplied the lacunae from Malone's complete text of the letter. The date is obviously 1697. It was first printed by Dr. Johnson in *Lives of the Poets.*

1. Dryden seems to have been a frequent visitor at Denham Court, the seat of Sir William Bowyer. Here he translated the first Georgic and most of the last Æneid. See his postscript to the *Virgil,* in Malone, III, 562.

2. This suggests that Tonson was maliciously impeding the correspondence between London and Rome. I believe it more likely that Tonson was careless in the choosing of the messengers he used to convey the poet's letters. In support of this suggestion see Letter 50, and the notes. The reason for the survival of this sole letter to Rome supports this suggestion: through Tonson and his messengers it never left England.

3. Apparently Dryden never completed the alteration: the play was neither performed nor published. In the British Museum, Add. MS. 28692, is one scene of the play, incorporated with Rochester's *Valentinian*. See Montague Summers, *The Playhouse of Pepys,* p. 179, and Allardyce Nicoll, "Dryden, Howard and Rochester," *Times Literary Supplement,* January 13, 1921.

4. The song was *Alexander's Feast.*

5. According to Malone, Orlando Bridgeman, grandson of Lord Keeper Bridgeman. He was one of the Stewards of the St. Cecilia's Feast in 1697. He also subscribed to the *Virgil.* I am unable to discover the connection of Lady Elizabeth Dryden to his parents.

6. Apparently his sons at Rome had advised him to compromise with William's government in order to obtain financial assistance. The wealthy Catholics seem not to have taken him up, for at the close of the letter he complains that those who should have been his friends are negligent of him.

7. Harry, I believe, was Erasmus Henry, the youngest son. My only clue for understanding these references to him is that he was in Rome studying for the priesthood. But there is no definite evidence that he ever took orders. Indeed, in 1706 he was a defendant in a Chancery suit (C. 5/261/34) brought by Grace Pickering, widow of Sir Henry Pickering. In the Bill he is described as "gentleman late of London."

In his Answer he describes himself as "son of John Drydon Gentleman deceased who was the eldest son of Mary Dryden one of the sisters and coheirs of Sir Henry Pickering." He also claims all or part of the estate as cousin and heir. In 1710 he inherited the title and estates of his uncle, but died within the year. It seems possible that he was in the army, for in Dryden family documents he is referred to as "Captain." See Malone, I, i, 427.

Letter 48 . . . page 96

In the William Andrews Clark Memorial Library. It was first printed by Malone. Though the date must be conjectural, December seems reasonable, since *Alexander's Feast*, written for the St. Cecilia's Day celebration in November, was now in press.

1. The mistake recorded here seems to have been Dryden's. There were at least three Greek courtesans named Lais. The third was contemporary with Alexander. Thais of course accompanied Alexander on his Asiatic campaign.

2. Tom Brown, so far as I can discover, did not publish a satire on Dryden at this time.

Letter 49 . . . page 97

I do not know the whereabouts of this letter. Through the kindness of Mr. James M. Osborn I am able to incorporate Malone's corrections for his projected second edition. It can be dated December, 1697, for the *Alexander's Feast* is now in print.

1. Sir Robert Howard's play, which he had mentioned in the letter to his sons.

2. Knightley Chetwood (1650-1720), Dean of Gloucester. See Letter 11, note 4.

Letter 50 . . . page 98

In the British Museum, Egerton MS. 2869, f. 34. It was first printed by Malone, who correctly dated it in December, 1697.

1. Lady Mary Chudleigh was an amateur poet, whom Dryden perhaps met during his visits to the Clifford estate, Ugbrooke Park, in Devon. Lady Mary was a neighbor of Lord Clifford and connected with him by marriage. She published *The Ladies Defence* in 1701, and *Poems on Several Occasions* in 1703, which contained a tribute to Dryden, "On his Excellent Translation of Virgil."

2. The *Virgil*, which was being corrected for the second edition.

3. The preface to the *Pastorals*, by Knightley Chetwood.

4. So far as I can discover, Tonson did not publish a translation of Ovid's *De Arte Amandi* in 1698.

5. Everingham had completed the printing before March 28, 1698; for on that date he rendered an account to Tonson of the amount of paper he had used. See my article, "The Publication and Profits of Dryden's *Virgil*," cited above.

6. Probably either Dr. Gibbons or Dr. Hobbs, both of whom Dryden mentions in his Postscript to the *Virgil* as having brought him back to health.

7. Charles returned to England in the following summer or early autumn.

8. Mr. Francia is mentioned by Narcissus Luttrell as being an eminent Jew. He was apparently an important shipping merchant. See Luttrell's *Brief Relation*, IV, 254.

9. I cannot identify Ferrard. He may have been a messenger of sorts.

10. In Letter 47 Dryden, writing to his sons, was inclined to agree with them that Tonson himself was responsible for the miscarriage of the letters between London and Rome.

Letter 51 . . . page 100

This letter was first printed by Mark Van Doren in *The Poetry of John Dryden* (New York, 1920). A copy of it is preserved in the Caryll-Pope correspondence in the British Museum, Add. MS. 28618, f. 84b, from which the present text is derived.

John Caryll (1666-1736) was the friend of Pope, who is remembered by the opening lines of *The Rape of the Lock*: "This verse to Caryll, Muse, is due." In 1697 Caryll succeeded to Ladyholt, the estate of Lord Caryll.

1. Whether he visited Caryll I do not know. His health must have improved, for he was visiting in Northamptonshire in late summer or early autumn of this year.

Letter 52 . . . page 101

This letter is in the possession of Mr. Oliver R. Barrett, of Chicago, Illinois, who very kindly allowed me a copy. It was first printed by Malone.

Mrs. Steward, who was one of Dryden's most faithful correspondents, was Elizabeth, daughter of John and Elizabeth Creed. Mrs. Creed was Dryden's cousin. Her daughter married Elmes Steward of Cotterstock about 1692. She was a talented woman, especially interested in painting.

1. He was apparently now at Tichmarsh, but whom he was visiting I do not know.

2. Charles, the eldest son, was home from Italy, and seems to have remained with his father until the latter's death. Charles survived his father only four years; he was drowned in the Thames, in 1704.

Letter 53 . . . page 102

In the collection of the Historical Society of Pennsylvania. The date is difficult to arrive at. I place it in October because in the preceding letter, to Mrs. Steward, he seems to suggest that he has plans for only ten days or two weeks more in the country before his return to London. This letter seems to me to be the last before he left Tichmarsh for the city. It was first printed by Malone.

1. Gerrard Street is between Leicester Square and Shaftesbury Avenue, and runs from Wardour Street to Greek Street. It was opened about 1681—only a few years before Dryden moved to it—and was named for Charles Gerard, first Earl of Macclesfield. See H. B. Wheatley, *London Past and Present*, II, 104.

2. John Creed, the father of Mrs. Steward, was made a Deputy Treasurer of the Fleet in 1660. Two years later he became Secretary to the Commissioners for Tangiers, and in 1663 he was elected to the Royal Society. He was closely associated with Pepys. In 1668 he married Elizabeth, daughter of Sir Gilbert Pickering, Dryden's uncle. On her mother's side, Mrs. Creed was a cousin of Pepys. In her old age, in 1722, she erected a monument to Dryden and his parents in Tichmarsh Church. See K. A. Esdaile, "Cousin to Pepys and Dryden: A Note on the Works of Mrs. Elizabeth Creed," *Burlington Magazine*, LXXVII (1940), 24-27.

3. Dorothy was a younger sister of Elizabeth Steward.

4. Pretty Miss Betty, Elizabeth Steward's first child, was now about four years old.

Letter 54 . . . page 103

In the William Andrews Clark Memorial Library. It was first printed by Malone.

1. Probably he means "to converse with."

Letter 55 . . . page 105

In the Pierpont Morgan Library. It was first printed by Malone.

1. John Creed.

2. The village of Cotterstock is a few miles northwest of Oundle.

Letter 56 . . . page 107

Printed first in the *Illustrated London News*, August 28, 1858, p. 197, from which I take the present text. The letter was prefaced with the following note: "By the kindness of a well-wisher we are this week enabled to publish, and for the first time, the recently-discovered letter from Dryden to the Duke of Ormond, of the Rebellion of 1715. It is a kind of begging-letter in the true Dryden manner." Saintsbury printed the letter in Volume XVIII, of his edition of Dryden, but he was not sure of its genuineness. I have no doubt that it is genuine.

Letter 57 . . . page 108

I do not know the whereabouts of this letter. Through the kindness of Mr. James M. Osborn I am able to incorporate Malone's corrections for his projected second edition.

1. I do not understand Dryden's reference. "Heer" seems to refer to a watering place and "them" to waters. He is obviously in London and intends to try the waters there before going to Bath. Possibly he had in mind Islington Spa, or New Tunbridge Wells, so-called because the quality of the waters was like that at Tunbridge. Islington Spa, for which 3d. was charged, was opened about 1685.

2. His *Fables* were published early in March, 1700, according to Malone (I, i, 327) on the authority of an advertisement in *The Flying Post*.

Letter 58 . . . page 110

In the Pierpont Morgan Library. It was first printed by Malone.

Letter 59 . . . page 112

In the Pierpont Morgan Library. It was first printed by Malone.

1. John Driden of Chesterton was at this time a Member of Parliament. His affection for the poet's family is partly shown by his bequest of £500 to Charles in 1707, but since Charles had predeceased him, it became a lapsed legacy.

2. This was possibly Beville Dryden, one of the sons of the first Sir John Dryden, the poet's uncle.

3. It came out two days after the writing of this letter—on March 6 in the *London Gazette*, No. 3,476, according to Malone.

4. Dr. Thomas Tennison, who had succeeded Tillotson in 1694.

5. The order, dated February 18, was printed in the *London Gazette* for Monday, February 27, 1698/9. Nahum Tate, the poet laureate, had

drawn up some proposals for the reformation of the stage on February 6. This document (Lambeth Palace Library, Vol. 933, item 57) was printed by Joseph Wood Krutch in *Comedy and Conscience after the Restoration* (New York, 1924).

6. The book of miscellanies, after many interruptions, was published in March, 1700, as *The Fables.*

Letter 60 . . . page 114

In the William Andrews Clark Memorial Library. It was first printed by Malone.

Letter 61 . . . page 115

First printed by Malone. It was then in the Pepysian Library at Magdalene College, Cambridge. Since my inquiries there remain unanswered, I use Malone's text.

1. Dryden's translations from Ovid, Boccaccio, and Chaucer included in *The Fables* were as follows: From Chaucer, *The Knight's Tale* (Palamon and Arcite), *The Nun's Priest's Tale*, *The Wife of Bath's Tale*, *The Flower and the Leaf* (then regarded as Chaucer's), and the Character of a Good Parson, Imitated. From Ovid's *Metamorphoses*, Meleager and Atalanta (Book VIII), Baucis and Philemon (Book VIII), Pygmalion and the Statue (Book X), Cinyras and Myrrha (Book X), Ceyx and Alcyone (Book XI), the whole of Book XII, Ajax and Ulysses (Book XIII), On the Pythagorean Philosophy (Book XV). From Boccaccio's *Decameron*, *Sigismonda and Guiscardo*, *Theodore and Honaria*, and *Cymon and Iphigenia.*

2. Most of the work on the *Fables* must have been completed by midsummer.

3. The friendliness of the letter suggests a closer relationship between Dryden and Pepys than has been supposed. Though Pepys mentions Dryden on several occasions in the *Diary*, only once is there an intimation of acquaintanceship at Cambridge, where they were contemporaries in the fifties.

Letter 62 . . . page 116

The whereabouts of this letter I do not know. Malone first printed it, but gave no indication of the source of his text, which I here reproduce.

1. Apparently Dryden was not the only antagonist of bad priests.

Letter 63 . . . page 117

In the William Andrews Clark Memorial Library. It was first printed by Malone.

Letter 64 . . . page 118

In the Pierpont Morgan Library. It was first printed by Malone.

1. Councillor Jennings I have been unable to identify.

2. Antigoo, i.e. Antigua, an island in British West Indies, the residence of the governor of the Leeward Islands.

3. This was Christopher Codrington. Born in Barbadoes, he was sent to England to be educated. In 1685 he entered Christ Church and in 1690 was elected a probationer fellow to All Souls. In 1694 he fought in Flanders with King William. Although he succeeded his father as captain-general of the Leeward Islands in 1697, he did not immediately take up residence in Antigua. Between 1696 and 1699 he was a man-about-town with some pretensions to wit and learning. He died in 1710 and in his will established Codrington College in Barbadoes. He was one of the subscribers to Dryden's *Virgil*.

4. This was probably Rose, two years younger than the poet, and the wife of John Laughton, D.D., of Catworth.

5. The wine from Ribadavia in Galicia was famous even in Elizabethan days. It was a very delicate, white, dry wine. Who Mr. Cole was I do not know.

Letter 65 . . . page 120

In the British Museum, Add. MS. 12112. Though undated, it was probably written, as Malone suggested, in October, 1699. I also accept Malone's attribution of it to Charles Montague, afterwards Earl of Halifax. In 1692 he had been appointed a lord of the Treasury. His greatest achievement was the formation of the Bank of England. As a reward for his brilliant organization he was made Chancellor of the Exchequer and a member of the Privy Council. In May, 1699, he was forced to resign as Chancellor; but on November 18, he was appointed Auditor.

1. The verses to his Cousin Driden, which were printed in the *Fables*.

2. These were to the Duchess of Ormond. In Letter 66, he tells Mrs. Steward that Montague has seen both the verses to Cousin Driden and those to the Duchess of Ormond.

3. By this time, the translation of the *Virgil* had assumed the proportions of a national achievement, and Dryden doubtless hoped to accomplish the same in translating Homer; but only a few months of life remained to him.

Letter 66 . . . page 121

In the Pierpont Morgan Library. It was first printed by Bell. It is undated by Dryden, but a later hand has written in pencil "Oct. 1699." It is written on the reverse of Charles Dryden's letter to Mrs. Steward, which is as follows:

Madam,

I have been so sensible of the loss of your Charming conversation ever since my departure, that I assure you in all my travells I never left any place with more reluctance than Cotterstock, and never found any satisfaction equall to what I enjoyd there. I have enclosd the papers which you were pleasd to lend me and have read them with extream pleasure, as I should receive any thing which comes from your fair hands. I heartily hope this may find you in better health, for as I am infinitely obligd, so nobody can wish your happiness in all respects more than my selfe. With my most humble service to my cousin Steward for all his favours I am, Madam,

Your most obedient humble servant
Charles Dryden

1. Dr. John Radcliffe was a popular and successful physician. He attended King William; and in 1705 he was called in to prescribe for the youthful Pope. Property left by him at his death in 1714 was employed by his executors in founding the Radcliffe Observatory and Library at Oxford. ,

Letter 67 . . . page 122

In the Pierpont Morgan Library. It is merely dated "Nov. 7th"; the year is obviously 1699. It was first printed by Malone.

1. There is no record of Dryden's attempts to get help from William's government. But it may be that Dorset, Montague, and others did solicit in his behalf.

2. If we can judge from this, and other statements in the letters, there is absolutely no doubt about Dryden's religious sincerity during the last years of his life.

3. *Friendship Improv'd;* or *the Female Warriour,* by Charles Hopkins. It was written in rime. *Boadicea* had been acted in 1697.

4. Dorset seems always to have been kind to Dryden. Legends about Dryden's wit and good humor at Dorset's dinners are recorded in Miss V. Sackville-West's *Knole and the Sackvilles* (London, 1922).

Letter 68 . . . page 125

First printed in *Miscellanea* (London, 1727), pp. 149-151. On page 147 of this edition is a separate title page: *Familiar Letters to Corinna by Mr. Dryden*. According to Malone (I, ii, 96) the letter is dated "Nov. 12, 1699" in the extract printed in *Memoirs of Pylades and Corinna* (1731). I retain this date. Elizabeth Thomas was a young woman of good family, who made Dryden's acquaintance in the last year of his life. Nearly thirty years later she provided the bookseller Curll with a very faulty account of Dryden's death and funeral, which was published in Curll's *Memoirs of Congreve*. Her story was generally accepted until Malone discredited a great deal of her testimony. See Malone, I, i, 347 ff.

1. Katherine Phillips. Her stepfather had first married Elizabeth Dryden, an aunt of the poet. See Philip W. Sowers, *The Matchless Orinda* (Cambridge, Mass., 1931).

2. This is an error. There is no evidence that Dryden ever lived in St. Giles in the Fields.

3. Count de Gabalis was the Abbé de Villars Montfaucon. In 1670 he published *Les entretiens du Comte de Gabalis sur les sciences*. It was reprinted in 1684. Pope found here some of the machinery of the elves and gnomes for *The Rape of the Lock*.

Letter 69 . . . page 127

First printed in *Miscellanea* (London, 1727), pp. 151-152. Malone's date of November, 1699, is probably correct.

1. In the preface to the *Fables*, Dryden publicly recants for his offenses against good taste: "I shall say the less of Mr. Collier [Jeremy Collier], because in many things he has taxed me justly; and I have pleaded guilty to all thoughts and expressions of mine, which can be truly argued of obscenity, prophaneness, or immorality, and retract them."

2. Creech translated Theocritus in 1682. Two years later he dedicated to Dryden his *Odes, Satyrs, and Epistles of Horace*.

Letter 70 . . . page 128

In the Pierpont Morgan Library. It was first printed by Malone.

1. Dryden probably means that Dennis, in the coffeehouses, recommends it to the town. In *The Life of Mr. John Dennis the Renowned Critic* (1734) the author says that Colonel Codrington prevailed on all his friends to take tickets for the poet's night (Allardyce Nicoll, *A History of Early Eighteenth Century Drama*, p. 18).

187

2. *Achilles, or Iphigenia in Aulis*, by Abel Bowyer. Though adapted from Racine, it contained many elements which characterize the English heroic play.

3. The Duchess of Norfolk was Mary, daughter of Henry Mordaunt, second Earl of Peterborough. She married the seventh Duke of Norfolk on August 8, 1677. He separated from her in 1685, and gained a divorce by Act of Parliament on April 11, 1700, on the grounds of her misconduct. She became *suo jure* Baroness Mordaunt in 1697. She died in 1701.

4. The Chancellor was John, Lord Somers. Though there was obviously no great friendship between him and Dryden, he was nevertheless a friend to many literary men at the turn of the century, and was a member of the Kit-Kat Club.

5. Erasmus Dryden, of King Street, Westminster. After the death of the poet's son, Erasmus Henry in 1710, this brother inherited the Dryden baronetcy and estates.

6. Jemima, Mrs. Steward's young daughter, who was baptized on February 25, 1697. See George Baker, *The History and Antiquities of the County of Northampton*, II, 298.

Letter 71 . . . page 130

In the Pierpont Morgan Library. It was first printed by Malone.

1. The *Fables*.

2. In the preceding letter Dryden had told her that Mr. Price reported that her father, John Creed, was to be made sheriff. Her husband, Elmes Steward, was to have the office.

3. See the preceding letter: the plays were by Dennis and Bowyer.

4. "In the London Gazette, No. 3557, Thursday, Dec. 14, 1699, it is mentioned that a Proclamation . . . had been issued out on the 11th instant" (Malone).

5. Dryden, it should be recalled, was a small landowner. From his father's estate he had inherited land near Blakesley, in Northamptonshire. See Letter 39, note 2.

Letter 72 . . . page 132

First printed in *Miscellanea* (London, 1727), p. 153.

1. Erysipelas.

2. Dryden complains in the preceding letter of Tonson's slowness in printing the *Fables*. It was finally issued in March, 1700.

Letter 73 . . . page 133

I do not know the whereabouts of this letter. Through the kindness of Mr. James M. Osborn I am able to incorporate Malone's corrections for his projected second edition.

1. "The Ballad of the Pews" was identified by Malone as "The Brawny Bishop's Complaint." It is an amusing satire on Bishop Burnet, who is represented as appealing to Princess Anne to stop the young ladies of the Court from ogling the gallants while he is trying to preach in St. James's Chapel. "The Confederates" deals with the presentation of Peter Motteux's adaptation of Fletcher's *Island Princess,* which was acted probably in December, 1698. The Confederates, among whom are those mentioned in this letter, gather to view the triumph of Motteux's opera. Walsh is not known to have written this piece.

2. Sir Thomas Skipwith, the patentee of the Theatre Royal.

3. Lord Scarsdale was Robert Leke, Earl of Scarsdale. He was interested in Anne Bracegirdle, the actress.

4. She was Mary Tudor, natural daughter of Charles II, by Mary Davies.

5. Francis, Lord Radcliffe, who became Earl of Derwentwater in 1696/7. In 1693 Dryden dedicated to him the *Examen Poeticum.* See Letter 26.

Letter 74 . . . page 134

In the Roberts Collection, Haverford College, Pa. It was first printed by Malone.

1. John Driden of Chesterton, Huntingdonshire. He was the second son of Dryden's uncle, Sir John Driden, and was at this time, and until his death in 1700, a Member of Parliament from Huntingdon.

2. The Statute, 11 and 12 William III, declared that after September 29, 1700, all papists who had not taken the oaths of allegiance and supremacy should be incapable of holding property or inheriting (Malone).

3. *The Way of the World.*

Letter 75 . . . page 135

In the Pierpont Morgan Library. It was first printed by Malone.

1. Sir John Vanbrugh, the dramatist and architect.

2. Dryden wrote the prologue, epilogue, and masque. It is doubtful, however, whether the play was acted before his death on May 1, 1700. It was published on June 18, according to Malone on the authority of the *London Gazette.*

3. The play, as printed, was called *The Fate of Capua.*

4. I am not certain how to interpret this sentence. Betterton was at this time manager of Lincoln's Inn Fields, whence he and the rebels who had broken with the United Company in 1695, had moved. But Dryden had apparently no connection with that company: the *Pilgrim*

was acted at Drury Lane. Was Dryden perhaps acting as a sort of consulting critic?

Letter 76 . . . page 137

In *An Useful and Entertaining Collection of Letters upon Various Subjects* (London, 1745), pp. 228-229. The date, though uncertain, was probably in the 1690's. Swan was a notorious punster of the time. Dryden refers to him in the *Discourse Concerning the Original and Progress of Satire* as follows: "A miserable clench, in my opinion, for Horace to record: I have heard honest Mr. Swan make many a better, and yet have had the grace to hold my countenance." Since this letter and the next contain nothing of importance and little of entertainment, and since their validity as correspondence may be questioned, I include them here merely for matter of record.

Letter 77 . . . page 138

In *Miscellaneous Letters and Essays on Several Subjects* . . . , ed. Charles Gildon (London, 1694), p. 1. I am indebted to James M. Osborn for drawing my attention to this letter and furnishing me a transcript.

INDEX

INDEX